# This Book
# Cooks

# This Book Cooks

A Caterer's Secret Collection

## Kerry Dunnington

*To our wonderful Sister! Merry, Merry Happy, Happy, We Love You, Kerry, Nick & Artichoke 2007 xoxo*

To order additional copies of this book, contact:
Xlibris Corporation
1-888-795-4274
www.Xlibris.com
Orders@Xlibris.com
26107

# Contents

## Elegant Main Dishes ................................................................72

## Miscellany ......................................................... 141

## Chocolate Desserts ............................................. 155

## Cakes, Pies, Cookies, Cookie Bars, And Surprises ...... 169

# Dog Treats ....................................................................... 193

This book is dedicated to
my husband, Nick, my mother, Joan
and our Norwich terrier, Artichoke
Isle of View


In memory of Eloise Weatherly
who loved books

# Acknowledgements

Many thanks to Nick, my wonderful husband, and everyday taste tester who was honest and encouraging. A big thank you to my mother, Joan and my sister, Kater, who shared with me invaluable hints, short cuts, and many of their signature recipes. Thank you Jane Cione for introducing me to Leslie Wiggins, my editor and indexer. To family, friends and all you taste testers for your support; you helped to make this project enlightening and fun.

I want to recognize as well, the following people who in some way contributed to this cookbook: Serena Baum, Dody Brager, Sandra Brookman, Penny Crawford, Joan D' Angelo, Mark Decker, Cathy Dryden, Ian and Renee Dunnington, Jane Durkee, Judy Gordan, Carolyn Gorman, Jeannie Jacobs, Jenny Johnson, Ester Jones, Kater Leatherman, Kim Leatherman, Kristan Leatherman, Dori Luneski, Mary Lee Lynch, Johanna McDill, Cindy Page, Phyllis Pullen, Jonni Ryan, Margaret Saccone, Mary Smith, Harvey Sugarman, Susie Vogelhut, Eloise Weatherly, Steve Wilhide and Virginia Wilkinson.

# Introduction

As you read the recipes in this cookbook, you will learn the type of cook I am, the kind of food I like, the way I enjoy entertaining and how preparing food is a passion and gift I adore.

I am a middle of the road kind of person; I want and like the best of both worlds. If canola or olive oil can be substituted for butter in a cake, and I can not identify the difference, why not?

I have enjoyed the work involved in compiling the recipes in this cookbook. I hope in some way you will not only benefit from preparing my recipes, but perhaps this collection will do for you what it did for me. It inspired me to share good, nutritional food with family, friends and clients.

Cheers and happy entertaining . . . .

# Tips, Alternatives and Suggestions

**Workspace** . . . . an uncluttered working space will allow you to focus clearly on the task before you and will give you the necessary freedom to prepare menus, lists, and food. Clean and clear your kitchen cabinets and pantry, and arrange your kitchen so that it works best for you. Frequently used items should be stored at your fingertips, if you are struggling to get to an item, then you are inviting unnecessary aggravation into your daily round. Dispose of any food or pantry items that you no longer eat. If for example, sardines have been keeping company in your pantry and you know you will never eat them, give them to the next food drive! Include the cleaning of your refrigerator in this mowing process and toss any old food and/or condiments.

**Sponges** . . . . are nesting places for all kinds of germs, before your "wiping" implement gets to looking like storm clouds, throw it in the washing machine, dishwasher or replace it.

**Reading recipes** . . . . before preparing any recipe, *always* read the entire ingredient list and thoroughly read the directions.

**Spices** . . . . I am fond of Vanns Spices (www.vannsspices.com) and honor the company's philosophy and the way in which they develop relationships with small farmers and choose top spice suppliers worldwide. Spices enhance, flavor, and add color to food, but they also do incredible things to our senses. If Vanns Spices are not available, use a good quality spice—preferably spices that have not been irradiated. Clean out your spice cabinet, get rid of anything that seems old. It is best to keep your spice collection in a cool dry place and certainly not above the stove!

**Salt** . . . . there is a difference in the quality and contents of table salts available for purchase. I prefer to use salt in its natural form, it makes a difference when seasoning food. Moreover, salt that is not bleached, kiln dried, heated or altered with pollutants or chemicals is better for your health.

**Dairy and non-dairy foods** . . . . if you are sensitive to dairy, you can (with almost the same flavor results) use soy or rice milk in recipes calling for milk. Throughout the cookbook, low fat versions of dairy are called for, if you want a richer flavor, regular may be used in place of reduced fat.

**Room Temperature** . . . . removing food from the refrigerator at least an hour or more before cooking or serving will have an over all affect on the way food cooks and tastes. A few variables to consider are the size of the item and the outside temperature. Use your own judgment, especially in the summer months or in a warm climate, and particularly with meat, poultry and dairy.

**Feta Cheese** . . . . there are various brands of feta cheese, my favorite and the one that is most often called for in the cookbook is Valbrasso. Cheese experts tell me that imported feta cheese has a more robust flavor then domestic. Whole Foods Market has a fabulous variety of Feta cheese, as do independent cheese shops.

**Bread** . . . . having read several versions about proofing yeast, kneading dough, bread equipment and so on, I thought I'd never bake a loaf of homemade bread. Here are some simple steps about the art of making a loaf of bread. The Goat Cheese and Olive Stuffed Bread recipe on page 125 is a good bread to start with. It is a small amount of dough to work with and the result is rewarding.

**Proofing Yeast** . . . . yeast has an expiration date, check the date and make certain your yeast is fresh. Yeast "grows" with the help of added sugar, a warm environment and a liquid that is warm. Always proof the yeast in a warm place that is free from drafts. Successful places to proof yeast are a sunny place, the top of a radiator or simmer a pot of water and let the yeast sit close by or place the bowl on top of the simmering water. If your kitchen is drafty, warm the area by setting your oven to the lowest temperature.

**Kneading** . . . . most loaves take about 10-15 minutes to knead. When I knead bread, I use it as a time to meditate, plan my day or week or reflect on a memorable moment. At first your hands will be sticky from the dough but as you gradually add flour and knead the dough your loaf will begin to become smooth and elastic, ready for its' first rising.

**Baking Bread** . . . . after the loaf has cooked according to directions and is nicely browned, and you're not certain if it is cooked through, tap the bottom of the loaf; if it sounds hollow, it is fully baked.

**Serving Sizes** . . . . when I plan a party, I prepare more than enough food to escape the distraction of all the worrying that comes along with having enough food for a party. If the food is delicious, people will indulge until they are more than full. Always, however, consider the number of guests, the time of day, the duration of the party and the time of year. A rule of thumb that works for me is to allow about three hors d'oeuvres per person. I round off my selection of hors d' oeuvres in odd numbers, three, five, seven and nine. Nine selections for parties of 60 or more, seven selections for parties of 40, five selections for parties of 25 and three selections for 15 people and under. After years of catering and hosting my own parties, this formula has been successful.

**Fruits and Vegetables** . . . . root vegetables can be tough, woody and strong-flavored, this is especially true with carrots, beets and parsnips. If available choose small fruits and vegetables, they are usually sweeter and tender. Grocery stores often rubber band certain produce items like lettuce, green onions and asparagus, this method of binding chokes the vegetable which often causes bruising. Unleash your purchases when you get home. Farmer's markets and vegetable stands on the side of the road and U-pick farms are a great way to utilize summer's bounty and can be a lot of fun. If you are interested in freezing or canning in large quantities this is the place for you.

**Organic** . . . . I support organic food and buy it when available. Chemicals are not an item I welcome into my body and although most of the chemical washes off when you wash with a fruit and vegetable wash, some still lingers.

**Seasonal** . . . . years ago, you could only buy fruits and vegetables when they were in season. For example, asparagus was seldom available unless it was springtime. Now, however, you can buy asparagus year round. I use vegetables and fruit when in season, it produces a more flavorful outcome in a recipe. Purchasing fruits and vegetables out of their growing season taxes the environment.

# Appetizers with Cheese

The meeter and greeter—or the first impression if you will. When planning the menu for a party, consider whether the appetizers will be passed, on a cocktail table or buffet table. Holding a drink in one hand and grasping a nibble with the other is tricky. To avoid having your guests feel awkward, tray and pass stationary food items and place dips, pates and tortes on a buffet or cocktail table. Appetizers that are unwieldy, too big and/or drippy are factors to consider when planning a party.

Cheese Curry Pate with Plum Sauce
Melted Swiss Dip
Feta "Dream" Cheese
Marinated Roquefort
Cheddar and Pecan Torte with Strawberry Preserves
Chipped Beef and Cheese with Walnuts
Smoked Salmon Pate
Cream Cheese Filled Vegetable Turnovers
Artichoke and Feta Melt
Supreme Cream of Crab Spread
Pecan Blue Cheese Crackers
Pepper Spread
Apricots and Cream with Teriyaki Walnuts
Pistachio-Gruyere Cheese Spread
Orange Marmalade Torte
Rice Crispy Wafers
Cheddar Cheese and Cauliflower Fritters
Pesto Cheese Torte
Marinated Brie with Peach Marmalade
Melted Cheese and Artichokes
Shrimp Dip
Pizzazzy Refried Bean Pate

# CHEESE CURRY PATE WITH PLUM SAUCE

## About 2 cups

This is a brilliant creation from my sister. The pate can be prepared one or two days in advance. The plum sauce recipe makes enough for two pates and will keep for several weeks in the refrigerator. The flavors in this creation are bold; it is best to serve with a bland cracker. The plum sauce is also delicious over baked chicken, broiled fish, and Brie cheese or as sauce for the Cream Cheese filled Vegetable Turnovers on page 9. This recipe doubles beautifully.

### PATE

One 8-ounce package light cream cheese, softened
1    cup sharp white cheddar cheese, shredded
2    tablespoons cooking sherry
1    teaspoon curry powder
Thinly sliced green onion for garnish

In a medium bowl, combine cream cheese, cheddar cheese, sherry and curry powder. Mix until thoroughly combined. To serve, shape mixture into a round about 6 inches in diameter and 1 ½ inches high. Cover tightly with plastic wrap until ready to serve.

### PLUM SAUCE

One 12-ounce jar plum preserves
1    tablespoon apple cider vinegar
1    tablespoon brown sugar
1    teaspoon red pepper flakes
1    clove garlic, minced
½    teaspoon powdered ginger

Combine all ingredients in a medium saucepan, bring to a boil, stir, remove from heat and allow to cool before storing in a jar. Just before serving spread half of the plum preserves over pate, top with chopped green onions and serve with crackers.

# MELTED SWISS DIP

## 1½ cup yield

People love the taste of this dip! It is so simple to prepare and usually I have the ingredients on hand. This recipe can easily be doubled or tripled.

1    cup grated low-fat Swiss cheese
1    cup chopped onion
⅓    cup mayonnaise

Preheat oven to 350. Combine all ingredients, spread in a casserole dish to accommodate and bake for 15 minutes or until light brown and bubbly. Serve with crackers.

# FETA "DREAM" CHEESE

## Yields about 2 cups

This savory combination is delicious and takes very little time to prepare. Serve with raw vegetables, won ton chips (recipe on page 144) or crisp crackers. I use Valbresso brand feta cheese; the flavor is among the best I have ever tasted.

1    clove garlic
1    cup feta cheese, crumbled
½    cup light cream cheese, softened
3    tablespoons olive oil
¼    cup Kalamata olives pitted
3    tablespoons chopped green onions
½    cup chopped walnuts

In a food processor, pulse garlic until minced, add feta, cream cheese, olive oil and olives, pulse until mixture is nearly smooth. Add onions and walnuts and pulse mixture until well blended. Chill for 2 hours or overnight before serving.

# MARINATED ROQUEFORT

## About 1½ cups

The amount of red onion called for in this recipe may seem excessive but all of it is necessary to pull off the full flavor. Prepare this several hours before you plan to serve it or make a day in advance. Serve with celery sticks, bite size tortilla chips or crispy crackers.

½   pound Roquefort, crumbled
1   medium red onion, cut in half and thinly sliced
¼   cup olive oil
1   tablespoon lemon juice
1   tablespoon red wine vinegar
2   cloves of garlic, minced
½   teaspoon dry mustard
½   teaspoon salt
½   teaspoon pepper

Assemble Roquefort in a 9-inch casserole dish and cover with red onion slices. In a medium bowl, whisk until fully combined, olive oil, lemon juice, vinegar, garlic, dry mustard, salt and pepper. Pour over cheese/onion mixture. Marinate for several hours or overnight. Serve at room temperature.

# CHEDDAR AND PECAN TORTE

# WITH STRAWBERRY PRESERVES

## About 6 cups

This simple to prepare torte is great to serve for large gatherings. Serve with crackers or fresh French bread rounds. A good quality or homemade strawberry preserve is recommended.

One-pound sharp white cheddar cheese, grated (5 cups)
1    cup pecans, chopped
¾   cup onion, minced
1    cup mayonnaise
Dash of cayenne pepper
A few sprinkles black pepper
One 12-ounce jar strawberry preserves
Chopped fresh chives or thinly sliced scallions for garnish

In a large bowl, combine cheddar cheese, pecans, onion, mayonnaise, cayenne and black pepper. Transfer to a serving platter and mold cheese into an oval shape. Using the scoop part of a soup ladle, mold an indentation in the center of the torte. Cover and chill. Allow torte to come to room temperature and just before serving, fill center and top with strawberry preserves and garnish with fresh chives or scallions.

# CHIPPED BEEF AND CHEESE

# WITH WALNUTS

## About 2 cups

This dip is creamy and salty and the walnuts give it just the right crunch. I serve this easy to prepare dip with a hearty shredded wheat type cracker.

One 8-ounce package light cream cheese, softened
2    tablespoons milk, any variety
½    cup light sour cream
2    tablespoons onion, chopped
1    package chipped beef, chopped
¼    cup walnuts, chopped

Preheat oven to 350. In a medium bowl, combine cream cheese, milk, sour cream, onion and chipped beef. Spoon mixture into a baking dish and top with walnuts. Bake for 15 minutes or until mixture bubbles slightly.

# SMOKED SALMON PATE

# Yields 3½ cups

The ricotta cheese in this flavorful salmon recipe makes it lighter than most versions. Vanns Spices Lemon and Dill seasoning works wonderfully, but dried dill works with almost the same results. Serve with dark pumpernickel bread, toasted pita wedges, or plain, thin crackers.

Two 8-ounce packages light cream cheese, softened
1    cup low-fat ricotta cheese
2    tablespoons cooking sherry
2    teaspoons fresh lemon juice
1    tablespoon onion flakes
2    teaspoons dried dill or Vanns Spices Lemon and Dill
½    teaspoon salt
Pepper to taste
4-ounces smoked salmon, chopped
Small capers and chopped red onion for garnish

In a medium bowl, combine cream cheese, ricotta cheese, sherry, lemon juice, onion flakes, dill, salt and pepper. Fold in smoked salmon and mold into a round, oval or square shape. Just before serving, generously garnish with capers and chopped red onion.

# CREAM CHEESE FILLED

# VEGETABLE TURNOVERS

## Yields 25 won ton triangles

These tasty morsels are crispy on the outside, creamy on the inside and the flavor is further enhanced if you top them with a dollop of your favorite preserve or jam.

4-ounces light cream cheese, softened
won ton wrappers, 25 count—about half a package
¼   cup scallions, thinly sliced (white and green part)
¼   cup carrot, minced or shredded
¼   cup zucchini, minced or shredded
A few dashes salt
Olive or Canola oil for frying
Preserves or jam

In a small bowl, combine cream cheese, scallions, carrot, zucchini and salt. Working with one won ton at a time, place about one teaspoon of the cream cheese mixture in the center of the won ton and fold over into a triangular shape. Dampen fingers with water and pinch seams together. Set won tons on a plate, placing wax paper or plastic wrap between each layer to prevent the won tons from sticking together. Continue filling each won ton wrapper until you have finished using the cream cheese mixture. In a large frying pan over medium high heat, heat oil, brown won tons for about 1-2 minutes on each side. Serve immediately.

# ARTICHOKE AND FETA MELT

## About 2½ cups

In the Renaissance times, artichokes were thought to be an aphrodisiac. It wasn't until the 16th century that they were fully introduced in France. The artichoke is a food all unto itself revealing a unique flavor, texture and appearance. Serve this tasty dip with tortilla chips, or a thin, crisp cracker and watch it disappear!

One 14-ounce can artichoke hearts drained and chopped
1    cup Feta cheese, crumbled
½    cup Parmesan cheese, grated
1    cup low fat mayonnaise
1    garlic clove, minced
¼    cup pimento drained and chopped

Preheat oven to 350. In a medium bowl, combine artichokes, Feta, Parmesan, mayonnaise, garlic and pimento. Spoon into a one-quart baking dish, bake for 30-45 minutes or until bubbly and light brown.

# SUPREME CREAM OF CRAB SPREAD

## As an appetizer for about 30-40 persons

Crabmeat differs in flavor, so you may need to adjust the seasonings in this recipe. A plain, bland cracker is a good choice for this spread.

Two 8-ounce packages light cream cheese, softened
1   cup low fat mayonnaise
½   cup light sour cream
2   tablespoons fresh lemon juice
¼   cup fresh, finely chopped parsley
¼   cup red pepper, minced
1   teaspoon Worcestershire sauce
Dash cayenne pepper
Dash Old Bay seasoning
2   pounds lump crabmeat, picked of shell

Preheat oven to 325. In a large bowl, combine until well blended, cream cheese, mayonnaise, sour cream, lemon juice, parsley, red pepper, Worcestershire sauce, cayenne and Old Bay. Fold crabmeat into cream cheese mixture. Bake for 45 minutes or until heated through.

# PECAN BLUE CHEESE CRACKERS

## About 70 thinly sliced crackers

This is great for a cocktail party and is delicious with a glass of white wine. I like to serve it in a pretty basket lined with a colorful napkin.

1   stick of butter, softened
½   pound Saga cheese, softened
1   egg, separated
1   cup white flour
1½  cups pecans toasted and finely chopped

In a medium bowl, cream butter and Saga cheese until smooth and well blended. Stir in egg yolk and flour; mix until well combined, add pecans. Divide the dough in half and form into two logs. Cover with plastic wrap and refrigerate overnight. This also may be frozen until ready to bake. Preheat oven to 375. Slice to desired thickness and place on a cookie sheet, brush with egg white and bake for about 12 minutes. Place on a rack to cool.

# PEPPER SPREAD

## About 2 cups

Every summer we buy several jars of homemade pepper jam from the local farmer's market. On a warm summer evening, I combined these ingredients and the result was a refreshing spread with lots of zip. Serve with a plain crisp cracker.

One 8-ounce package light cream cheese, softened
1    cup shredded sharp white cheddar cheese
⅓    cup pepper jam
2    tablespoons sherry
A    few dashes Tabasco sauce

In a food processor, combine cream cheese, cheddar cheese, pepper jam, sherry and Tabasco sauce, process until smooth.

# APRICOTS AND CREAM WITH TERIYAKI WALNUTS

## Yields about 50 pieces

These tasty, bite size morsels are a different twist from the usual fare served at cocktail parties. They also make a great bite size dessert. Choose dried apricots that give to the touch. You may prepare the cream cheese mixture in advance and spoon onto the apricot, top with the walnut, however, just before serving.

| | |
|---|---|
| 2 | cups walnut halves |
| ⅓ | cup soy sauce or tamari |
| 3 | tablespoons dark rum |
| 2 | tablespoons toasted sesame oil |
| 1 | clove garlic, crushed |
| 1 | teaspoon ground ginger |
| 4-6 | drops Tabasco sauce or hot pepper sauce |
| 1 | tablespoon brown sugar |

Salt to taste
One 8-ounce package light cream cheese, softened

| | |
|---|---|
| 4 | teaspoons apricot jam |
| 1 | tablespoon Amaretto |
| 1 | pound halved dried apricots |

Preheat oven to 350. In a medium saucepan, combine soy sauce or tamari, rum, sesame oil, garlic, ginger, Tabasco or pepper sauce and brown sugar. Over moderate heat, cook mixture until sugar dissolves, stirring constantly. Remove from heat and toss in walnuts, stir to combine well, spread nuts on a lightly oiled cookie sheet, and bake for 15 minutes. Check halfway through baking time to make sure they do not burn. Transfer to an oiled sheet of tin foil and season with salt. In a small bowl, combine cream cheese, apricot jam and Amaretto. Spoon about a teaspoon of cream cheese mixture onto each apricot and top with a teriyaki walnut.

# PISTACHIO-GRUYERE CHEESE SPREAD

## About 3 cups

The union of white wine, pistachio nuts and lemon rind gives this recipe an unusual flavor. Serve with crackers.

⅓   cup low fat or regular mayonnaise
2    cups Gruyere or Swiss cheese, shredded
3    tablespoons white wine
¼    teaspoon Dijon mustard
¼    teaspoon garlic powder
2    tablespoons fresh onion, minced
½    cup pistachio nuts, chopped
2    tablespoons parsley, minced
1    teaspoon lemon rind, grated

In a medium bowl, combine mayonnaise, cheese, white wine, Dijon mustard, garlic powder and onion. In a small bowl, combine pistachio nuts, parsley and lemon rind. Place cheese mixture in serving bowl and top with pistachio mixture. Serve at room temperature.

# ORANGE MARMALADE TORTE

## About 4 cups

A good quality and chunky orange marmalade is recommended for this recipe. This delicious torte can be prepared one or two days in advance.

2     tablespoons mayonnaise
1     teaspoon Dijon mustard
Two 8-ounce packages light cream cheese, softened
1     cup shredded white cheddar cheese
⅔    cup fresh pineapple, chopped
1     teaspoon dried mint
¾    cup chopped pecans, toasted
1⅓   cups chunky orange marmalade, divided
¼    cup dried cranberries for garnish
¼    cup thinly sliced green onion for garnish
Ginger snaps

In a small bowl, combine mayonnaise and mustard, set aside. In a food processor, combine one package cream cheese, ½ of the mayonnaise/mustard mixture, cheddar cheese, pineapple and mint, process until well blended. Line a 6-inch mold with plastic wrap making certain that there is ample plastic wrap to hang over the sides. Spread the pecans evenly over the plastic wrap then spread the cream cheese mixture over pecans. Process the remaining 8-ounce package cream cheese with the mayonnaise/mustard mixture and ⅓ cup of the orange marmalade until smooth. Spread evenly over cream cheese mixture. Cover and refrigerate. To serve, remove mold by pulling up the plastic wrap, invert to a platter and garnish with remaining orange marmalade, dried cranberries and sliced green onions.

# RICE CRISPY WAFERS

## About 3 cups

Another great, make ahead, easy to prepare party nibble. These crispy wafers have a wonderful flavor and texture. I like their informal ragged edge appearance.

1   stick of butter, softened
1   cup grated sharp white cheddar cheese
1   cup rice crispies
¾   cup white flour
¼   cup wheat germ
Pinch of salt
Dash of Tabasco or hot pepper sauce

Preheat oven to 350. In a medium bowl cream the butter, add the cheese, and mix well. Add rice crispies, flour, wheat germ, salt and Tabasco or hot pepper sauce and combine until thoroughly blended, dough may be a bit stiff. Knead for a few minutes until well incorporated. Pinch off bite size pieces and place on an ungreased cookie sheet. With the back of a three-prong fork, make an indentation in the dough. Bake for 15-18 minutes, cool on wire rack before serving.

# CHEDDAR CHEESE

# AND CAULIFLOWER FRITTERS

## About 16-20 fritters

These fritters are like peanuts, eat one and you will eat them all! Dip them in warm maple syrup or for a more robust flavor, accompany the fritters with a spicy chili and garlic puree found in the specialty aisle of the grocery store.

1½    cups white flour
2      teaspoons baking powder
½     teaspoon salt
2      cups diced cauliflower
1      cup shredded sharp cheddar cheese
1      tablespoon onion, minced
1      egg
1      cup skim or low-fat milk
Canola oil for cooking

In a large bowl, combine the flour, baking powder and salt. Stir in cauliflower, cheese and onion. In a small bowl, whisk together the egg and milk and add to the flour mixture, stir just to combine. In a medium skillet over moderately high heat, heat about 1 tablespoon of the canola oil. Drop tablespoons of batter into oil and cook for about 1-2 minutes on each side or until golden.

# PESTO CHEESE TORTE

## About 2 cups

This make-ahead party appetizer is especially pretty around the Christmas holidays. Serve with a bland cracker.

One 8-ounce package light cream cheese, softened
½  cup Roquefort cheese, crumbled, at room temperature
Pesto (recipe on page 154)
½  cup slivered sun-dried tomatoes

In a small bowl, combine cream cheese and Roquefort. Line a 5-6 inch round or square container with plastic wrap, allow enough plastic wrap to hang over the sides. Spread one third of cheese mixture over the bottom of the container. Spread ½ the pesto mixture over cheese, and sprinkle with sun-dried tomatoes. Repeat, finishing with the cheese. Cover and allow flavors to mingle for 24 hours. Invert to a serving platter and serve at room temperature.

# MARINATED BRIE

# WITH PEACH MARMALADE

## One 6-inch round

The creamy Brie soaks up the flavorful peach brandy, making this a taste treat combination. I use the peach marmalade (recipe on page 149) but any peach marmalade will work. For optimum flavor, marinate the Brie for 24 hours.

One 6-inch round of Brie cheese
2    tablespoons peach brandy
½    cup peach marmalade

Place Brie in a 6-inch round casserole dish. Fork score the Brie in several places and pour brandy over Brie, marinate for 24 hours. Allow Brie to come to room temperature. Preheat oven to 350. Spoon marmalade over cheese and bake for 25 minutes. Serve with crackers.

# MELTED CHEESE AND ARTICHOKES

## About 3 cups

I lightened the traditional version of this recipe. Serve this dip with an airy, crisp cracker.

One 15-ounce can artichoke hearts, drained and chopped
½   cup fresh grated Parmesan cheese
1   cup low fat, part skim Mozzarella cheese, shredded
½   cup light mayonnaise

Preheat oven to 350. In a medium bowl, combine artichoke hearts, Parmesan cheese, Mozzarella cheese and mayonnaise. Spread mixture in a 1-quart baking dish and bake for 35-45 minutes or until the top is light brown and the cheese is bubbling.

# SHRIMP DIP

## About 3 cups

For optimum flavor, prepare this dip a day in advance. Serve with a bland cracker.

One 8-ounce package light cream cheese, softened
Juice of one lemon
⅓   cup onion, chopped
2    tablespoons mayonnaise
1    teaspoon salt
Pepper to taste
Dash of Worcestershire sauce
1    teaspoon sugar
¾    pound cooked shrimp, peeled, deveined and chopped

In a medium bowl, combine cream cheese, lemon juice, onion, mayonnaise, salt, pepper, Worcestershire sauce and sugar. Beat with an electric mixer until well combined. Fold in shrimp, spoon into serving dish, cover and chill overnight.

# PIZZAZZY REFRIED BEAN PATE

## About 6½ cups

Bite size tortilla chips are perfect for dipping.


2     medium ripe, avocados
One 16-ounce can refried beans
One 12-ounce jar hot salsa
Juice from a ½ of a lime
1     cup light sour cream
1     cup shredded Monterey Jack cheese
1     medium shallot, minced

In a medium bowl, mash avocados with a fork, add refried beans, salsa, lime juice, sour cream, Monterey Jack cheese and shallot, combine well. Allow flavors to mellow for 2 hours or more before serving.

# Appetizers without Cheese

In addition to an appetizer with cheese, I like to offer one or two appetizers without cheese and I always coordinate my appetizer choices around the entire menu. For example, if I were serving the Apricot Meatballs as an appetizer, I would not choose the Tamale Pie as an entrée, too much meat. Once I have decided the type of party I am hosting, I consider key factors to making the party successful. Consider the time of year, (people eat more in colder climates), the number of guests, (the larger the party the more people eat), the duration of the party, (longer hours require more food). The time of day is a consideration as well (if you plan a brunch it is likely your guests did not have breakfast), and lastly, the age of your guests, (young adults, especially men have huge appetites). Approximations on serving sizes for appetizers are available in Tips, Alternatives and Suggestions.

Apricot Meatballs
Miracle Whipped Shrimp
Bacon Wrapped Breadsticks
Jumbo Marinated Shrimp
Creamy Bean Spread
Smoked Fish Dip
Avocado Pate
Caponata

# APRICOT MEATBALLS

## Yields about 60-70 bite size meatballs

People devour these meatballs! The meatballs and apricot sauce may be prepared one or two days in advance. Combine the two, however, *just* before baking.

2    pounds ground chuck
1    cup whole-wheat herb flavored bread crumbs
2    eggs, lightly beaten
Salt and pepper to taste
One 8-ounce bottle French dressing (Annie's Natural brand is
     delicious)
1    cup apricot preserves
1    envelope onion soup mix

Preheat oven to 350. In a medium bowl, combine ground chuck, bread crumbs, eggs, salt and pepper, mix thoroughly. Shape mixture into desired size balls. In a sauté pan, over moderate heat, brown the meatballs evenly on all sides. Transfer to a baking dish, allow to cool. In a medium bowl, combine French dressing, apricot preserves and onion soup mix. Pour over meatballs, cover and bake for 30-40 minutes or until sauce is bubbling.

# MIRACLE WHIPPED SHRIMP

## Serves 4 as a first course luncheon dish
or
## 8-10 as an appetizer

The secret to the savory flavor of this shrimp recipe is Miracle Whip salad dressing. For optimum flavor, make a day in advance. Crispy wheat crackers are best if serving as a dip. If serving as a first course luncheon dish, serve the shrimp with the Cucumber Bisque recipe on page 36.

¾   cup Miracle Whip salad dressing
1    teaspoon Worcestershire sauce
¾    teaspoon garlic, minced
¼    teaspoon Tabasco or pepper sauce or to taste
½    teaspoon lemon peel, minced
1    pound large shrimp, steamed, peeled, deveined and cut
     lengthwise
½    large onion, thinly sliced

In a small bowl, combine Miracle Whip, Worcestershire sauce, garlic, Tabasco and lemon peel. In a medium bowl combine shrimp and onion, toss with dressing.

# BACON WRAPPED BREADSTICKS

## 12 Servings*

These breadsticks are a great choice for a cocktail party. They are simple to prepare, and easy to eat. I have experimented with several types and brands of breadsticks and found the Stella Dora brand works best. Choose boxes with breadsticks that have not been broken.

1½  pounds bacon (about)
2    boxes Stella Dora breadsticks

Preheat oven to 350. In a spiral fashion, wrap one slice of bacon around each breadstick. Line breadsticks one-inch apart in a single layer on a baking sheet. Bake for about 15 minutes, turn and bake for an additional 10 minutes or until bacon is cooked *just* crispy. Allow breadsticks to cool slightly before serving.

*    2 breadsticks per person.

# JUMBO MARINATED SHRIMP

## Serves 30*

This shrimp is abundant with so much flavor that it does not require a dipping sauce.

5      pounds large or jumbo shrimp steamed, peeled and deveined
1      cup *fresh* lemon juice (about 6-8 lemons)
½      cup canola oil
2      tablespoons rice vinegar
2      cloves garlic, crushed
8-10 drops Tabasco or hot pepper sauce
2      tablespoons dry mustard
2      tablespoons salt

In a large bowl, whisk until well blended the lemon juice, oil, vinegar, garlic and Tabasco sauce. In a small bowl, combine the mustard and salt, slowly whisk into lemon/oil mixture. Pour over shrimp distributing evenly and marinate for 4-6 hours. Drain marinade before serving.

*      5 pounds of 16-20 count shrimp yields *about* 90 pieces of shrimp. For a cocktail party, allow about three shrimp per person.

# CREAMY BEAN SPREAD

## Yields about 1¾ cups

This is quick, easy to prepare and nutritional. Toasted French bread rounds that have been brushed with olive oil, tortilla chips or fresh crisp vegetables are great accompaniments.

1      clove garlic
¼     cup onion
¼     cup chopped parsley
One 15-ounce can white kidney beans, drained (liquid may be used
       as a broth in soups)
2      tablespoons fresh lemon juice
½     teaspoon pepper
½     teaspoon salt
½     cup chopped red pepper

In a food processor, combine garlic, onion, parsley, white kidney beans, lemon juice, pepper, and salt, pulse mixture until smooth. Stir in red pepper.

# SMOKED FISH DIP

# Yields about 3 cups

Prepare this a day in advance or the morning you serve it to allow the intense flavors to mingle. Small leaves of Belgian endive or crispy crackers are flattering accompaniments.

½   pound boneless smoked white fish (skin removed) crumbled into bite size pieces
½   cup fresh tomato, seeded and finely diced (about 1 medium)
⅓   cup thinly sliced scallions, green part only
⅓   cup fresh horseradish peeled and finely grated
¼   cup low fat sour cream
¼   cup low fat mayonnaise
¼   cup fresh lime juice

In a medium bowl, combine fish, tomato, scallions, and horseradish. In a small bowl, stir together sour cream, mayonnaise and lime juice, add to fish mixture and fold to combine.

# AVOCADO PATE

## About 1 cup

A simple and nutritious pate that is delicious served with tortilla chips, or for a different twist, serve the pate with the Jumbo Marinated Shrimp recipe on page 28.

1 ripe avocado, mashed (reserve pit)
1½ tablespoons fresh lemon juice
¼ cup onion, minced
1 tablespoon chopped green chilies
1 medium tomato chopped or a ¼ cup salsa
1 clove garlic, minced
¼ teaspoon salt or more to taste

In a medium bowl or food processor, combine until well blended, avocado, lemon juice, onion, green chilies, tomato or salsa, garlic and salt. To avoid discoloration place the avocado pit in the pate, remove just before serving.

# CAPONATA

## About 4 cups

The versatile flavor of this spread intensifies with age. I use it as an accompaniment to scrambled eggs, steak sandwiches and for a most memorable grilled cheese sandwich (recipe on page 111).

1    medium unpeeled eggplant cut into ½-inch slices
Olive oil
1    cup finely chopped celery, about 2 stalks
½    cup finely chopped onion
2    cloves garlic, minced
1    cup fresh tomato, chopped
3    tablespoons tomato sauce (any variety)
2    tablespoons seasoned rice vinegar
½    cup Kalamata olives pitted and chopped
2    tablespoons small capers
1    teaspoon sugar
¼    teaspoon salt or more to taste
¼    teaspoon pepper
2    tablespoons chopped fresh parsley

Preheat oven to 500. Arrange eggplant on a baking sheet; brush both sides with olive oil. Bake for 15 minutes, turning halfway through cooking time. Cool and cut into small chunks. In a sauté pan over medium heat, heat oil, add celery, onion and garlic, sauté for about 5 minutes stirring frequently. Add fresh tomato, tomato sauce, rice vinegar, olives, capers, sugar, salt and pepper, reduce heat to low and cook for an additional 10 minutes. Remove from heat and stir in eggplant and parsley. Allow to cool before serving. Serve at room temperature.

# Soups

It seems the most successful and appreciated dinner parties are when I serve soup as a first course, or especially if I host a soup sampling party! There are really two types of soup and both are featured in this chapter, a hearty meal-in-a-bowl variety served with a crusty loaf of bread or a light, slip-down-your-throat pureed type accompanied by a tossed salad. If serving soup as a first course (guests really appreciate this effort), serve one of the pureed soups; a lighter version that is welcome when you are about to eat a complete meal.

Wedding Soup
Cucumber Bisque
Carrot Vichyssoise
Grilled Hamburger Soup
Peanut Soup with Vegetables
Butternut Squash Soup
Canadian Cheese Soup
Vegetable Bisque
Chicken Soup with Cornmeal Dumplings
Sweet Pea Soup
Tofu, Leek and Prune Soup

# WEDDING SOUP

## Serves 4-6

A hearty soup that is both unusual and delicious. Complimentary accompaniments are the Delicious Biscuits on page 121 or the Butternut Squash Bread on page 134.

## MEATBALLS

½   pound ground chuck
1   egg, lightly beaten
Salt and pepper to taste
1   tablespoon fresh parsley
1   teaspoon minced dried onion
¼   teaspoon garlic powder
⅛   cup white or whole wheat bread crumbs

## SOUP

1   cup tofu cut into chunks or 1 cup cooked white meat chicken cut
    into bite size pieces
3   cans (14.25 ounce) low fat chicken broth
2   medium carrots, julienned
2   stalks celery, chopped
½   cup onion, chopped
1   tablespoon fresh parsley, minced
1 bunch fresh spinach, cooked, drained and chopped or one box frozen spinach completely thawed and drained of all liquid
Salt and pepper to taste
2   eggs, lightly beaten
3   tablespoons grated Parmesan cheese

In a medium bowl, combine ground chuck, egg, salt, pepper, parsley, onion, garlic powder and bread crumbs. Shape into small, bite size meatballs. In a sauté pan over medium heat, cook meatballs until light brown and cooked through. Set aside. In a large soup pot, bring chicken broth to a boil, add carrots, celery and onion, reduce heat to medium, cover and cook for about 5 minutes or until vegetables are fork tender. Add meatballs, tofu or chicken, parsley and spinach, season with salt and pepper. In a small bowl, whisk together beaten eggs and Parmesan cheese; set aside. Bring the soup back to a boil, add egg/Parmesan mixture, DO NOT STIR, cover, and reduce heat to simmer and cook for 3 minutes. Ladle soup into bowls, making certain each serving gets the egg/Parmesan mixture.

# CUCUMBER BISQUE

# Serves 6

Cucumbers really don't have any redeeming qualities when it comes to nutrition but when summer rounds the corner presenting itself with cucumbers aplenty, this soup is always on my list of summer must haves! It is best made a day in advance. Complimentary accompaniments are any of the cold shrimp entrees featured in the Elegant Main Dish section or sliced tomatoes, deviled eggs and a loaf of fresh crusty bread.

1   tablespoon butter
1   cup chopped onion
2   teaspoons flour
1   cup chicken broth
2   medium cucumbers, peeled and sliced (about 3 cups) plus extra
    cucumbers for garnish
1   cup plain non-fat yogurt
2   teaspoons chopped fresh parsley
½   teaspoon salt
Fresh cracked black pepper to taste

In a medium pot, over moderate heat sauté onion in butter until transparent. Whisk in flour and slowly add chicken broth. Stir until mixture is well combined. Add cucumbers, cover and bring to a boil, reduce heat and simmer for 45 minutes. Remove from heat and cool completely. In a food processor puree the cucumber mixture. Add the yogurt, parsley, salt and pepper; puree again until velvety smooth. Refrigerate for several hours or overnight. Garnish with cucumber slivers.

# CARROT VICHYSSOISE

## Serves 4

Beautiful in color, velvet in texture, divine in flavor. This is a lovely first course dish that may be prepared a day or so in advance.

2    tablespoons butter
1    medium onion, sliced
2    cups chicken broth
2    cups carrots, cooked and sliced
½    teaspoon salt
⅛    teaspoon black pepper
½    cup skim milk, low-fat, or regular milk
1    tablespoon parsley

In a medium pot, melt butter over moderate heat and sauté onion for about 5 minutes. Add 1 cup of broth and bring to a boil. Add carrots, cover, reduce heat and simmer for 15 minutes. Allow soup to cool slightly. Place mixture in a food processor, add remaining cup of chicken broth and season with salt and pepper, puree until smooth. Stir in milk. Garnish with parsley.

# GRILLED HAMBURGER SOUP

## Serves 6-8

I developed this soup from a refrigerator full of leftovers. If you do not have leftover hamburgers use about 1½ pounds lean ground chuck. Vegetable Soup-N-Stock is a delicious seasoning similar to bouillon and is available in the spice aisle at a health food or specialty store. This soup is delicious with the Muenster bread recipe on page 130.

1   medium onion, chopped
6   leftover hamburgers or 1½ pounds lean ground chuck
5   cups water
4   teaspoons Vegetable Soup-N-Stock
1   medium carrot, shredded
2   medium tomatoes, chopped
1½  cups broccoli, cooked until tender and chopped
2   cups cooked Basmati rice
Fresh ground black pepper to taste

In a medium skillet, sauté onion over moderate heat until translucent. If using raw ground chuck add to the sautéed onions and cook until light brown, drain off any fat. In a large pot bring water to a boil and stir in Vegetable Soup-N-Stock, leftover hamburgers or cooked ground chuck, carrots, tomatoes, broccoli, and rice. Bring to a second boil, cover, reduce heat and simmer for 10 minutes, season with black pepper.

# PEANUT BUTTER SOUP

# WITH VEGETABLES

## Serves 6

This delicious and unusual soup is hearty enough to be served as a main dish.

Olive oil

1    cup sweet potato, peeled and cubed
½    cup onion, chopped
½    cup diced red pepper
1    clove garlic, minced
1    cup salsa (medium heat)
1    can chicken broth (14.25 ounce)
1    cup cooked white rice
¾    cup black beans, drained (liquid may be used as additional stock in another soup)
1    cup extra firm tofu or cooked white meat chicken or shrimp that has been steamed, peeled and deveined, cut into bite size pieces
¼    cup chunky peanut butter

In a large pot, heat olive oil over moderate heat and sauté sweet potato, onion, red pepper and garlic, sauté for about 5 minutes. Stir in salsa, chicken broth, rice and beans. Bring to a boil, reduce heat to simmer, add tofu, chicken or shrimp. Whisk in peanut butter. Simmer for 10 minutes. Serve immediately.

# BUTTERNUT SQUASH SOUP

## Serves 12-15

My cousin, Steve Wilhide hosted a dinner for us one evening and served this velvety smooth, sunset colored, comforting soup as a first course. It could however, be served as a luncheon main dish with the Muenster bread recipe on page 130, or as a light supper entrée.

3    leeks, white part only, thinly sliced
2    large onions, diced
4    tablespoons butter
2    teaspoons curry powder
5    cans (14.25 ounce) low fat chicken broth
4    large Idaho baking potatoes, peeled and cubed
2    medium butternut squash, peeled, seeded and diced
Salt and pepper to taste
Green onion, thinly sliced

In a large pot, melt butter over medium heat and sauté leeks and onion until glossy. Add curry and sauté until fragrant, a minute or so; add chicken broth, potatoes and butternut squash, bring mixture to a boil, reduce heat and simmer for 1 hour or until vegetables are fork tender. When soup has cooled, puree in a food processor until it has the consistency of heavy cream. Garnish bowls with green onion.

# CANADIAN CHEESE SOUP

## Serves 6

There are many varieties of cheddar cheese; sharp aged white cheddar works well in this recipe. Serve with any of the hearty vegetable salads beginning on page 47 and a loaf of fresh crispy French bread.

2 large potatoes, diced
½ cup celery, chopped (about 1 stalk)
½ cup carrots, chopped (about 1 medium)
½ cup onion chopped
1 teaspoon olive oil
2 cans (14.25 ounce) low fat chicken broth
Salt and pepper to taste
⅓ cup skim milk
½ pound shredded sharp cheddar cheese

Place potatoes, celery and carrots in a large pot and *just* cover the vegetables with salted water. Bring mixture to a boil and simmer until vegetables are soft. Sauté onion in oil until translucent, add to cooked vegetables along with chicken broth and bring to a boil, reduce heat and simmer for 10 minutes. In a food processor, puree soup, return to pot and season with salt and pepper. Add milk and *slowly* stir in cheese, cook on a low heat until cheese has melted.

# VEGETABLE BISQUE

## Serves 20

This is a great soup to prepare when autumn's harvest is abundant with vegetables.

1    stick, plus 2 tablespoons butter
2    medium onions, sliced
2    leeks, sliced (white part only)
7    cups low fat chicken broth
1    cup white wine
½    cup sherry
1½   cups tomato puree
2    cups carrots, sliced
2    cups potatoes, peeled and diced
1    cup cauliflower florets cut into bite size pieces
2    cups celery, sliced
3    cups unpeeled zucchini, sliced
2    cups acorn squash, peeled, seeded and diced
Salt and pepper to taste
Chopped fresh parsley for garnish

In a medium skillet over moderate heat, melt butter, add onion and leeks, sauté until onions are transparent. Transfer onions to a large pot. Add chicken broth, white wine and sherry, bring to a boil and stir in tomato puree. Add carrots, potatoes, cauliflower, celery, zucchini, acorn squash, and salt and pepper. Cover, reduce heat and simmer until vegetables are tender. In a food processor, puree soup until smooth, adjust seasonings, garnish with parsley.

# CHICKEN SOUP WITH CORNMEAL DUMPLINGS

## Serves 4

This recipe is an adaptation from the soup my grandmother often prepared for our family.

## SOUP

Olive oil
1    medium onion, chopped
2    skinned, boned chicken breasts (about 1 pound)
2    cans (14.25 ounce) low fat chicken broth
1    cup chopped carrots (about 2 medium)
1    cup celery, thinly sliced (about 2 stalks)
¼    cup parsley, minced
Salt and pepper to taste

In a large pot, heat olive oil over moderate heat and sauté onion until translucent. Add chicken and broth, bring mixture to a boil, cover and reduce heat to simmer and cook for 15 minutes. Remove chicken breasts, when cool enough to handle cut into bite size pieces. Return chicken to the pot, add carrots, celery, and parsley, season with salt and pepper, bring to a boil, cover, reduce heat to simmer and cook for about 10 minutes or until vegetables are cooked.

## DUMPLINGS

## Yields about sixteen 1-inch dumplings

½    cup yellow cornmeal

½    cup flour
1    teaspoon baking powder
½    teaspoon salt
⅛    teaspoon pepper

⅛   cup water
2   teaspoons olive oil
1   egg, lightly beaten

In a medium bowl, combine cornmeal, flour, baking powder, salt and pepper. Whisk in water, olive oil and egg. Shape into 1-inch balls. Add dumplings one at a time into about 2 quarts of water that has boiled and *then been brought back to a simmer*. Cover and cook for 10 minutes remove with a slotted spoon and add to chicken soup just before serving.

# SWEET PEA SOUP

# Serves 10

This recipe is simplistic in its ingredients as well as its preparation. For a lovely luncheon or summer supper, serve with the Curry-Cashew Tuna Salad on page 102.

6    tablespoons butter
1½   cups onion, chopped
7    cups frozen sweet peas
2    cans (14.25 ounce) chicken broth
Salt and pepper to taste

In a medium pot over moderate heat, melt butter and sauté onion until translucent. Add peas and chicken broth, bring to a boil and reduce heat to simmer and cook for 20 minutes. Allow soup to cool and puree in food processor until velvety smooth, season with salt and pepper.

# TOFU, LEEK AND PRUNE SOUP

## Serves 2

I am fond of the simplicity of tofu. That may seem unusual coming from a cook who loves flavorful food, but there is something about this non-descript, good-for-you food that appeals to me. If you are not a fan of tofu, cooked white meat chicken may be substituted for the tofu.

1    cup leeks, white part only, thinly sliced
½   teaspoon olive oil
1    can (14.25 ounce) chicken broth
6    pitted prunes cut into thirds
1    cup extra firm tofu cut into bite size cubes or cooked white meat
     chicken
2    tablespoons chopped parsley
½   teaspoon dark sesame oil
½   teaspoon tamari or soy sauce
Salt and pepper to taste
2    tablespoons cooked wild rice, optional

In a medium pot over moderate heat, sauté leeks in olive oil until lightly browned. Add chicken broth and bring mixture to a boil, reduce heat and stir in prunes, tofu or chicken, parsley, sesame oil, tamari, salt, pepper and wild rice if desired. Serve immediately.

# Salads and Side Dishes

Many of the recipes in this chapter were created (resulting from the only food choices I had in the refrigerator) to offer texture, color, balance, variety, flavor and nutrition. Some need nothing more than bread as an accompaniment while others make a delicious addition to seafood, chicken and meat. Complimentary accompaniments are offered throughout the chapter for easy menu planning.

Celery Almandine
Zucchini "Slaw"
Red Cabbage Salad
Baked Summer Vegetables
Green Beans with Spiced Walnuts and Feta
Orange Marmalade Tomatoes
Broccoli, Sweet Onion and Cashew Salad
Peanut Coleslaw
Brandied Carrots with Peas
Stuffed Lettuce
Marinated Potato Salad
Baked Spinach with Cheese
Vegetarian Delight
Golden Rice Salad
Carrot and Leek Gratin
Bacon Stuffed Potatoes
Mango and Cashew Salad with Lime Dressing
Seasoned Tomato Casserole
Creamy Mashed Potatoes
Marinated Onion "Slaw"
Bloody Mary Aspic
Addictive Potato Salad
Rainbow Salad

# CELERY ALMANDINE

## Serves 2-4

This dish is a taste treat and one made complete if served with baked chicken and steamed rice.

⅓   cup slivered almonds
2   tablespoons butter
4   cups sliced celery (slice diagonally about ¼ inch thick)
½   cup chicken broth
1   tablespoon dried minced onion
½   teaspoon garlic powder
½   teaspoon powdered ginger
2   teaspoons soy sauce

In a medium sauté pan over moderate heat, melt the butter and add the slivered almonds, sauté until light brown, stirring often. Watch closely so they don't burn. Add celery, chicken broth, minced onion, garlic powder, ginger and soy sauce, stir to combine ingredients. Cover, reduce heat to medium-low and cook celery for 10-20 minutes or until tender, stirring once or twice during the cooking time.

# ZUCCHINI "SLAW"

## Serves 4-6

The secret to this delicious dish is the warm dressing tossed with the room temperature vegetables. Prepare the dressing and toss the salad just before serving. To round out the meal, serve with the Sesame Pork Tenderloin on page 91 and the Marinated Potato Salad on page 58.

2   medium zucchini unpeeled and cut into thin julienne strips
1   small red pepper, cut into thin julienne strips
2   medium shallots, thinly sliced
4   tablespoons olive oil
4   tablespoons walnuts, chopped
2   tablespoons seasoned rice vinegar
1   teaspoon sugar
Salt and pepper to taste

In a large bowl toss together zucchini, red pepper and shallots. In a sauté pan over medium heat, heat oil and sauté walnuts for about 5 minutes, stirring frequently so as not to burn the walnuts. Remove from heat and stir in vinegar, sugar, salt and pepper. Pour over zucchini and toss; serve immediately.

# RED CABBAGE SALAD

## Serves 4-6

The dictionary defines purple as an emblem of royalty or high rank. My tasters said this salad was as delicious as it was beautiful. Toss the salad with the dressing just before serving.

5   cups red cabbage, shredded
⅓   cup raisins
⅓   cup walnuts coarsely chopped and toasted
⅓   cup thinly sliced green onions
½   cup Roquefort cheese, crumbled
Salt and pepper to taste
Celery Seed Dressing (page 145)

In a medium bowl, combine cabbage, raisins, walnuts, green onions and Roquefort, toss with celery seed dressing, season with salt and pepper.

# BAKED SUMMER VEGETABLES

## Serves 10-12

When tomatoes, zucchini and potatoes are at their peak in summer, I like to prepare this simple, colorful and tasty dish. It is delicious served with chicken, fish, meat or pork. It also makes a wonderful accompaniment to scrambled eggs.

4 tablespoons olive oil
6 small to medium potatoes, about 1½ pounds, thinly sliced
2 medium zucchini, thinly sliced
3-4 ripe tomatoes, sliced
3 cloves garlic, minced
Coarse salt, to taste
Coarsely ground black pepper, to taste
Chopped fresh parsley for garnish

Preheat oven to 350. Lightly oil a 9x13-inch baking dish with 1 tablespoon olive oil. Lay sliced potatoes along entire bottom of baking dish, overlapping the slices by half. Drizzle with 1 tablespoon olive oil and sprinkle with salt and pepper. Cover the potatoes with the zucchini slices overlapping by half. Drizzle with another tablespoon of olive oil, sprinkle with salt, pepper and garlic. Cover the zucchini with the tomatoes, drizzle with remaining tablespoon of olive oil, salt and pepper. Cover and bake for 50-60 minutes or until potatoes are tender when pierced with a knife. Garnish with parsley.

# GREEN BEANS
# WITH SPICED WALNUTS AND FETA
## Serves 4

This side dish is abundant with flavor and color and is delicious served with chicken, pork or beef.

1    tablespoon soy sauce or tamari
1    tablespoon dark rum
1    tablespoon toasted sesame oil
2    tablespoons brown sugar
¼    teaspoon ground ginger
½    cup walnut halves
1    pound green beans, washed, trimmed and steamed or cooked until desired tenderness, keep at room temperature
½    cup dried cranberries
1    cup feta cheese crumbled, at room temperature

Preheat oven to 375 degrees. In a small bowl, combine, soy sauce or tamari, rum, sesame oil, brown sugar and ground ginger. Add walnuts and toss well, making certain to coat nuts well. Place on a foil lined cookie sheet and bake for 10 minutes, cool. In a large bowl, toss green beans, cranberries, feta cheese, and walnuts. Serve immediately.

# ORANGE MARMALADE TOMATOES

## Serves 6

If fresh summer tomatoes are not available, substitute one 28-ounce can of chopped tomatoes and omit the cup of tomato juice. This dish is a delicious companion to the Broccoli, Sweet Onion and Cashew salad on page 54 and the Cheese Casserole recipe on page 76.

2   tablespoons butter
1   teaspoon curry powder
1   cup onion, chopped
1   cup tomato juice
½   cup orange marmalade
1   teaspoon cinnamon
Salt and pepper to taste
6   large ripe tomatoes, cored, seeded, tops removed and skinned*
     or one 28-ounce can chopped tomatoes

Preheat oven to 350. In a sauté pan over moderate heat melt butter and add curry powder, stir for a minute or so, add onion and sauté for 5 minutes or until softened. Add tomato juice, orange marmalade and cinnamon, (and can of tomatoes if not using fresh) bring mixture to a boil and remove from heat; season with salt and pepper. In a baking dish that accommodates the tomatoes, place fresh tomatoes core side up, pour sauce over top of tomatoes and bake uncovered for 45 minutes.

\*    To remove the skin from a tomato, plunge the whole tomato in boiling water for one minute, remove with a slotted spoon, allow to cool slightly and gently pinch off skin.

# BROCCOLI, SWEET ONION AND CASHEW

# SALAD

## Serves 4

The secret is to cook the broccoli until *just* fork tender, under cooked or over cooked broccoli will result in a *completely* different salad. Sweet onion, such as Vidalia contributes to the wonderful flavor in this salad. This dish is not a good keeper; serve immediately after you have tossed it with the dressing.

## SALAD

3   cups broccoli with stem, cut into small florets
½   cup sweet onion, thinly sliced
¼   cup red pepper, chopped
½   cup cashew pieces, roasted and salted
¼   cup raisins

## DRESSING

1   clove garlic, minced
1   tablespoon rice vinegar
1   tablespoon olive oil
1   tablespoon mayonnaise
1   teaspoon sugar
1   teaspoon tamari or soy sauce
Fresh ground black pepper to taste

In a medium pot, bring water to a boil, add broccoli, reduce heat and cook until *just* tender. Drain broccoli in a colander and run cold water through the broccoli until it has cooled. Transfer to a medium bowl and set aside, keep at room temperature. Add onion and red pepper. In a small bowl whisk together garlic, vinegar, olive oil, mayonnaise, sugar, tamari and black pepper. Toss dressing with broccoli, onion and red pepper stir in cashews and raisins. Serve immediately.

# PEANUT COLESLAW

## Serves 12-15

This coleslaw has a nice crunch quality, partly due to the addition of peanuts. The cayenne pepper gives this coleslaw a lot of zing, so to mellow the flavors, prepare the dressing a day in advance. If you are sensitive to pepper, reduce the amount of cayenne to a ¼ teaspoon. Cabbage varies in size, to prepare enough coleslaw called for in this recipe allow about 20 good size handfuls of the shredded cabbage. Keep in mind that cabbage shrinks after it has been dressed. Top with peanuts *just* before serving.

¾    cup plain low fat yogurt
¾    cup mayonnaise
1    tablespoon dark sesame oil
¼    cup apple cider vinegar
½    of a medium red onion, cut into chunks
1    teaspoon celery seed
½    teaspoon cayenne pepper
½    teaspoon black pepper
1    teaspoon salt
1    tablespoon sugar
1    medium head of green cabbage, shredded
1    small to medium head of red cabbage, shredded
6    carrots, peeled and grated
1    cup peanuts, roasted

In a food processor, combine the yogurt, mayonnaise, sesame oil, cider vinegar and red onion; puree until smooth. Add the celery seed, cayenne pepper, black pepper, salt and sugar, blend until all ingredients are incorporated. In a large bowl, toss green cabbage, red cabbage and carrots, pour dressing over cabbage, stir to combine. Top with peanuts just before serving.

# BRANDIED CARROTS WITH PEAS

# Serves 8

This combination is delicious! It is so simple to prepare, can be made in advance, is a complimentary accompaniment to seafood, chicken and beef and if you're planning a large party it doubles beautifully, what more could you ask for?

8    large carrots peeled and cut into julienne strips
¼    cup butter (½ stick)
2    tablespoons sugar
½    teaspoon salt
⅓    cup brandy
1    cup thawed green peas

Preheat oven to 350. Place the carrots in a 2-quart baking dish. In a medium saucepan, melt the butter over medium heat, add sugar, salt and brandy, pour over carrots and bake covered for 45 minutes or until carrots are tender. Toss peas with carrots *just* before serving.

# STUFFED LETTUCE

## Serves 6-8*

This is a fun recipe to prepare and one of the few lettuce salads that is dressed *and* can be prepared in advance, thus making this a good selection if you are planning a dinner party. Top each wedge with fresh ground pepper and if desired, homemade seasoned croutons. Any of the beef, potato and tomato dishes are complimentary accompaniments to this salad.

1   large compact head of lettuce
6-ounces light cream cheese, softened
⅓   cup blue cheese, crumbled
¼   cup mayonnaise
2   tablespoons green pepper, finely chopped
2   tablespoons red onion, finely chopped
2   tablespoons chopped chives
3   tablespoons walnuts, finely chopped
1   teaspoon Worcestershire sauce
½   teaspoon salt
A few dashes Tabasco sauce or any hot sauce
Croutons if desired

To remove the center core from a head of lettuce, bang the head against a hard surface and pull out core. Wash the lettuce by running cold water into the center of the lettuce head for a few minutes, invert and allow water to drain from lettuce for about 30 minutes. Hollow out center of lettuce (reserving lettuce for another salad) leaving a shell of about one inch. In a medium bowl, beat cream cheese, blue cheese and mayonnaise until smooth. Add green pepper, red onion, chives, walnuts, Worcestershire sauce, salt and hot sauce. Mix until well blended. Spoon mixture into center of lettuce, cover and refrigerate for several hours. To serve cut into wedges, top with fresh ground pepper and croutons if desired.

* Depends on the size wedge

58 KERRY DUNNINGTON

# MARINATED POTATO SALAD

## Serves 6

This potato salad only has 1 *tablespoon* of mayonnaise! For maximum flavor prepare this the day before you plan to serve it. Peeling the potatoes is a matter of preference.

6   medium potatoes, unpeeled, quartered and cooked in boiling salted water for about 15 minutes or until tender
1½  cups onion, quartered and thinly sliced
½   cup canola oil
¼   cup seasoned rice vinegar
1   teaspoon celery seed
1   teaspoon salt, or more to taste
¾   teaspoon black pepper
1   tablespoon mayonnaise

After potatoes have cooled completely, thinly slice. In a medium jar, with a tight fitting lid, combine oil, vinegar, celery seed, salt and pepper. With jar top on tightly, shake vigorously and allow dressing to stand at room temperature for several hours. In the dish you will be serving the potato salad, layer the potatoes and the onions alternately, pour the dressing evenly over the salad. Just before serving, toss the salad with the mayonnaise.

# BAKED SPINACH WITH CHEESE

## Serves 8*

For an elegant and delicious meal, I like to serve this spinach dish with the Marinated Beef Tenderloin on page 89 or the Broiled Oriental Flank Steak recipe on page 75 and the Bacon Stuffed Potatoes on page 63. For optimum flavor, prepare a day in advance.

1    medium onion, finely chopped
½    cup feta cheese, crumbled
½    cup Edam cheese, grated
¼    cup blue cheese, crumbled
¼    teaspoon ground nutmeg
2    tablespoons bread crumbs
3    tablespoons olive oil
2    packages frozen, chopped spinach thawed and drained
2    tablespoons grated Parmesan cheese

Preheat oven to 350. Oil a 10-inch baking dish. In a medium bowl, combine onion, feta, Edam and blue cheeses, nutmeg, breadcrumbs, and olive oil. Arrange spinach in baking dish, top with cheese mixture and sprinkle with Parmesan. Bake for 20-30 minutes. Broil to brown top.

*    If you want to serve this as an appetizer; fill phyllo cups (found in the frozen food section of the grocery store) three quarters full with spinach, top with cheese mixture and bake for about 10 minutes in a 350 oven.

# VEGETARIAN DELIGHT

## Serves 6

In my early twenties, I worked in a restaurant owned by an energetic man named Harvey Sugarman. He had nouveau thoughts about food and the way people wanted to eat and dine. The vegetarian delight was among his most popular menu selections. The beauty of this dish is its versatility, just about any vegetable works—if you don't have one of the vegetables called for in this recipe be creative and replace it with another of your favorites. Hardier vegetables require longer cooking times than the more delicate vegetables.

2    cups carrots, julienned (2 large)
2    cups cauliflower florets broken or cut into small bite size pieces
2    cups broccoli florets broken or cut into bite size pieces
1½ cups zucchini, quartered and cut into ½ inch thick pieces (1 small)
2    cups yellow squash, sliced into ½ inch rounds (1 medium)
2    cups celery sliced ¼ inch thick
1    large onion cut into chunks
Old Bay Seasoning (about 1 teaspoon)
⅓   cup freshly grated Parmesan cheese
2    cups shredded cheese, use one or any mixture of, Mozzarella, Monterey Jack or sharp white Cheddar

In a large pot with a steamer, bring water to a boil. Steam the carrots, cauliflower and broccoli, steam until *not yet fork tender*. Add zucchini, yellow squash, celery and onion, cook until desired tenderness. Transfer to a large bowl, gently toss and spoon into a baking dish, generously sprinkle the vegetables with Old Bay seasoning, top with Parmesan and shredded cheeses. Place baking dish under broiler and broil until cheese melts and turns a light golden brown.

# GOLDEN RICE SALAD

# Serves 6

For a complete meal, I serve this delicious salad with sautéed tofu or baked chicken. If mangoes are not ripe when purchased, allow 3-4 days to ripen, a consideration when planning to prepare this recipe. To get the flesh of the mango, cut lengthwise as close to the pit as possible. Score cut sides of each piece in a crosshatch pattern, turn it inside out, slice the mango from the skin.

1    tablespoon olive oil
1    tablespoon curry powder
1    teaspoon salt
2    cups cauliflower cut into small bite size pieces
¼    cup dried cranberries
¼    cup water
3    cups cooked Jasmati, Basmati or Texmati rice
½    cup cashews or almonds, toasted
1    cup ripe mango, peeled and cut into bite size pieces
3    tablespoons chopped fresh chives or thinly sliced green onion
¼    teaspoon black pepper

In a medium skillet over low heat, heat olive oil, add curry powder and cook until fragrant, about 1-2 minutes. Add salt and cauliflower stirring constantly until curry powder adheres to cauliflower. Add dried cranberries and a ¼ cup of water, cover and cook until cauliflower is just tender (or desired tenderness) about 5-15 minutes. In a large mixing bowl, combine rice, cauliflower mixture, cashews or almonds, mango, chives and black pepper. Toss ingredients until well distributed and allow to stand at room temperature for a ½ hour or more before serving.

# CARROT AND LEEK GRATIN

## Serves 6-8

A delicious side dish that is so versatile it may be served with beef, lamb, pork or chicken. Although five tablespoons of horseradish seems excessive, it gives this dish a wonderful flavor. The gratin can be baked in advance and reheated before serving time*.

2    tablespoons butter
4    cups shredded carrots (about 6 medium carrots)
2    cups sliced leeks, white parts only (about 4-5 medium leeks)
5    tablespoons prepared horseradish
1    teaspoon salt
A few grindings of fresh black pepper
1    cup whipping cream
1    cup low fat or 2% milk
2    eggs
½    cup shredded white cheddar cheese
⅓    cup breadcrumbs

Preheat oven to 350. Lightly cover a 2-quart baking dish with cooking spray. In a large skillet over moderate heat, melt butter and sauté carrots and leeks until softened about 4-5 minutes. Remove from heat and stir in horseradish, salt and pepper, transfer mixture to baking dish. In a medium bowl, whisk together cream, milk and eggs, pour over carrot/leek mixture and stir to combine. In a small bowl, combine breadcrumbs and cheese, set aside. Bake gratin for 30 minutes. Remove from oven and evenly distribute the breadcrumb/cheese mixture and bake for an additional 25 minutes.

*    To reheat gratin, allow dish to come to room temperature and heat for 15-30 minutes in a 350 oven.

# BACON STUFFED POTATOES

## Serves 8

A great side to serve when entertaining. Prepare them in advance and heat them just before serving. Beef makes a complimentary accompaniment to these potatoes.

4    baking potatoes
4    bacon slices cooked until crisp
½    cup low fat sour cream
½    cup shredded white cheddar cheese
⅓    cup chopped green onion
¼    cup milk
¼    teaspoon salt or to taste
Pepper to taste
2    tablespoons butter or better butter (recipe on page 142)
½    cup low fat buttermilk or substitute ½ cup milk to which you
     have added 1 teaspoon lemon juice

Preheat oven to 350. Bake potatoes for 1 hour or until fork slides through the center easily. When cool enough to handle, cut them in half and scoop out the pulp and place in a large bowl, mash the potatoes. In a medium bowl, combine sour cream, cheddar cheese, green onion, milk, salt, pepper, butter, buttermilk and bacon. Combine with the mashed potatoes and mix well. For creamier potatoes, adjust the amounts of sour cream, milk and/or buttermilk. Spoon potato mixture into shells, place on a baking sheet and bake in a 350 oven for 20-30 minutes. Adjust oven temperature to broil and lightly brown the top of potatoes.

# MANGO AND CASHEW SALAD

# WITH LIME DRESSING

## Serves 6

The combination of the sweet mango, the crunchy cashews and the salty lime dressing makes for an impressive and unusual lettuce salad.

## DRESSING

⅓    cup olive oil
¼    cup fresh lime juice
1    teaspoon salt

## SALAD

6    servings washed red leaf lettuce torn into bite size pieces
1    ripe mango, cut into bite size pieces*
1    can (14.4 ounce) hearts of palm, sliced
½    cup roasted cashews

In an 8-ounce jar, combine the olive oil, lime juice and salt, shake until well blended. Place lettuce leaves in a large bowl. In a small bowl, combine mango, hearts of palm and cashews, toss with dressing to coat. Toss lettuce leaves with enough dressing to coat. Divide lettuce among 6 serving plates. Top with mango mixture, distributing ingredients evenly, serve immediately.

*    To prepare a mango refer to the recipe on page 61

# SEASONED TOMATO CASSEROLE

## Serves 8-10

This recipe is easy to prepare, great for company, and is a complimentary accompaniment to red meat. The bread crumbs have a marvelous way of soaking up the liquid, so the result is more like a pudding.

1   stick butter (½ cup)
1   large onion, chopped
2   cans (28-ounce) whole tomatoes, pulled apart
¼   cup sugar
About 7 drops Tabasco
½   teaspoon curry powder
Salt and pepper to taste
1½  cups seasoned bread crumbs

Preheat oven to 350. In a medium sauté pan over medium heat, melt butter and sauté onion until translucent. In the casserole dish you will be baking the tomatoes, combine onion, tomatoes, sugar, Tabasco, curry powder, salt, and pepper. Top tomatoes with bread crumbs and bake uncovered for 1 hour.

# CREAMY MASHED POTATOES*

# 12 servings

The secret to the wonderful flavor in this recipe is the dried minced onion.

5 pounds potatoes, quartered and peeled if desired, reserve potato water
One 8-ounce package light cream cheese
1 cup light sour cream
2 tablespoons butter, softened
2 tablespoons dried minced onion
1 teaspoon salt
Pepper to taste

In a large pot, bring salted water to a boil, add potatoes, allow water to return to a boil, cover, and reduce heat to medium and cook potatoes until fork tender, about 20-30 minutes. In a medium bowl, beat until well-blended cream cheese, sour cream, butter, minced onion, salt and pepper. In a large bowl, mash potatoes with electric beater until *almost* creamy adding potato water if necessary to get the desired creaminess. Add the cream cheese mixture and beat (do not over beat) until ingredients are blended. Season to taste with salt and pepper. Serve immediately.

* To prepare stuffed baked potatoes, bake six potatoes in a preheated 400 oven for one hour or until tender when pierced with a fork. When cool enough to handle scoop out pulp and with an electric beater mash until almost creamy adding milk or potato water to get the desired creaminess. In a medium bowl, beat until well-blended, cream cheese, sour cream, butter, minced onion, salt and pepper. Fold in potatoes and beat until creamy. Spoon mixture into potato skins. When ready to serve, heat potatoes in a preheated 350 oven for 45 minutes to an hour or until hot. This version can be prepared in advance.

# MARINATED ONION "SLAW"

## Serves 4

These cold, crunchy marinated onions make for a delicious companion to beef, spare ribs and baked or grilled chicken.

2  medium sweet onions, cut in half, cut halves into thin slices, about 2 cups
¼  cup apple cider vinegar
¼  cup water
¼  cup sugar
¼  cup mayonnaise
¼  teaspoon celery seeds

In a medium bowl, combine vinegar, water and sugar, allow sugar to dissolve for about 15 minutes. Toss in onions and marinate for 8 hours or overnight. Drain onions, discarding marinade. In a small bowl, combine mayonnaise and celery seeds. Gently toss onions with dressing.

# BLOODY MARY ASPIC

## Serves 8

Alcohol is not an ingredient in this flavorful aspic, but I felt compelled to name this Bloody Mary aspic because the combination of lemon, horseradish and Worcestershire remind me of this Sunday brunch libation. If you are planning a dinner party, enhancing accompaniments are Seafood Newberg, page 97, Stuffed Chicken Breasts, page 95 or the Broiled Oriental Flank Steak on page 75. The decorative ½ cup individual molds are festive for a dinner party or if you are having a buffet, use a one-quart mold. Prepare this the day before you plan to serve it.

3    cups tomato juice
2    three-ounce packages lemon Jell-O
2    tablespoons apple cider vinegar
1    tablespoon horseradish
2    teaspoons Worcestershire sauce

Oil mold or molds with cooking spray. In a medium saucepan, slowly bring tomato juice to a boil, stir in Jell-O, vinegar, horseradish and Worcestershire sauce. Remove from heat and stir until the sugar from the Jell-O has dissolved. Pour into mold or molds. If using individual ½ cup molds fill each mold about three quarters full. To remove aspic, set mold or molds into hot but not boiling water for a few minutes and invert onto a plate or platter.

# ADDICTIVE POTATO SALAD

# Serves 20

This salad is a good choice for a potluck party, picnic or luncheon. You can cook the potatoes, boil the eggs and prepare the dressing in advance. Combine the remaining ingredients and toss the salad the day you plan to serve it. Whole Food Market's brand of mayonnaise has a consistency similar to thick salad dressing and its' flavor closely resembles homemade mayonnaise, however, other brands of mayonnaise work nearly as well.

## DRESSING

1½ cups mayonnaise
3 tablespoons apple cider vinegar
2 tablespoons sugar
1 tablespoon Dijon mustard
2 tablespoons celery seeds
Fresh black pepper to taste

## SALAD

4½ pounds whole (about golf ball size) red potatoes, unpeeled
2½ cups chopped celery
½ cup small capers
1 cup pimento stuffed green olives sliced into thirds
1 cup chopped green onions
1 cup chopped sweet gherkins
6 hard boiled eggs, chopped

In a medium bowl, combine mayonnaise, vinegar, sugar, mustard, celery seeds and pepper, whisk until smooth. Cover and refrigerate. In a large pot, cover whole potatoes with cold water and place over medium high heat. When water comes to a boil, lower heat to medium (water should be dancing) and cook potatoes until fork tender, about 20-30 minutes. Drain and allow potatoes to cool completely. When cool, cut potatoes into bite size pieces and place in a large bowl. In a medium bowl, combine celery, capers, green olives, green onions, sweet gherkins and eggs. Add to potatoes and toss with dressing. Cover and refrigerate for at least 2 hours before serving.

# RAINBOW SALAD

## Serves 4-6

If you are looking to prepare a salad with lots of flavor, color and texture, you have met your match with this delicious combination. Valbresso brand Feta cheese is a tangy feta that works well in this salad.

4   cups shredded purple cabbage
1   cup ripe mango* cut into small chunks
1   ripe avocado, cut into bite size pieces (prepare just before serving)
½   red pepper, cut into bite size pieces
2   green onions, thinly sliced
½   cup Valbresso Feta cheese, crumbled
½   cup roasted and salted cashews
Celery Seed Dressing, recipe on page 145
Salt and pepper to taste

In a large bowl, gently toss the cabbage, mango, avocado, red pepper and green onions. Lightly coat salad with dressing and toss to combine evenly. Toss in Feta cheese and cashews, season with salt and pepper. Serve immediately.

*    To get the flesh of a mango, cut lengthwise as close to the pit as possible, score cut sides of each piece in a crosshatch pattern, turn it inside out, then cut the mango from the skin.

# Elegant Main Dishes

Entrees are one of the most important food selections when entertaining; in fact, it is central to my planning the menu. The collection in this chapter offers several elegant choices for entertaining. Many recipes can be prepared in advance, a welcome feature when entertaining. In the introduction, several recipes feature salads and side dishes that compliment the entrees as well as a wine suggestion.

Pear, Pork and Soba Noodle Salad

Broiled Oriental Flank Steak

Cheese Casserole

Summertime Tomato Pie

Greek Shrimp Salad

Creamy Chicken and Zucchini Casserole

Marinated Sea Island Shrimp

Beef Tenderloin with Blue Cheese Stuffing

Basil Shrimp Pasta

Brisket

Mediterranean Shrimp

Seafood Lasagna

Marinated Beef Tenderloin

Sesame Pork Tenderloin with Mustard Cream

Shrimp with Lemon and Garlic

Hot Seafood Salad

Stuffed Chicken Breasts

Seafood Newberg

# PEAR, PORK AND SOBA NOODLE SALAD

## Serves 4-6

This unusual combination is lovely to serve as a luncheon entree. Marinate and cook the pork the day before you plan to serve the dish. Pork tenderloin comes packaged in a pair, marinate both tenderloins and use the other for another meal. The pears should be firm but fragrant. Soba noodles can be found along with other pasta products in most grocery stores.

Complementing wine: Red Zinfandel or Australian Shiraz

## DRESSING

3    tablespoons canola oil
4    teaspoons Dijon mustard
2    tablespoons seasoned rice vinegar
2    tablespoons soy sauce
2    tablespoons dark sesame oil

## SALAD

1    package Soba noodles, broken in half, cooked according to package directions and cooled
½    cup green onions, white and green part, sliced
1    red pepper, diced
1    marinated pork tenderloin*, cooked and sliced
2    pears, firm but ripe, peeled, cored and cubed (prepare pear *just before serving*)
2    tablespoons toasted sesame seeds

Place the cooled noodles in a large serving bowl. In a small bowl, combine canola oil, Dijon mustard, vinegar, soy sauce and sesame oil; whisk until well combined. Pour over noodles, add green onions and red pepper, marinate at room temperature for 2 hours.

Just before serving toss noodles with room temperature pork, pears and sesame seeds.

*　Marinate the meat with the sesame pork tenderloin recipe, (page 91), omitting the sesame seeds if desired.

# BROILED ORIENTAL FLANK STEAK

## Serves 4

This steak is delicious with the Potato Salad on page 58 and the Green Beans with Feta and Walnuts on page 52. The marinade can be used as a sauce, bring to a full boil before serving.

Complementing wine: Red Zinfandel or a fruity Shiraz

1¼   pound lean flank steak
¼    cup cooking sherry
¼    cup soy sauce
¼    cup honey
2    tablespoons white vinegar
1    tablespoon fresh gingerroot, minced
1    teaspoon dark sesame oil
2    cloves garlic, crushed

In a baking dish to accommodate the steak, combine the sherry, soy sauce, honey, vinegar, gingerroot, sesame oil and garlic. Place the steak in the marinade turning to coat, marinate for 8 hours. Turn steak occasionally to marinate evenly. Preheat oven and set on broil. Place steak on a rack and broil 7-8 minutes on each side for medium rare. Allow steak to cool for 5 minutes and slice thinly on the diagonal, serve with marinade if desired.

# CHEESE CASSEROLE

## Serves 6

I served this at a luncheon with the Orange Marmalade Tomatoes on page 53 and the Broccoli, Sweet Onion and Cashew Salad on page 54, the serving plate was abundant with color and my guests said the combination of flavors was extraordinaire! *It has to be prepared the day before and must be removed from the refrigerator 2 hours before baking.* A good quality Italian or French bread works well in this recipe.

Complementing wine: Beaujolais Grand Cru, such as a Flurie

4   cups day old white bread, (with crusts) lightly buttered and cut into cubes
2   cups grated sharp cheddar cheese
4   eggs, lightly beaten
2½  cups cows milk, any variety
½   teaspoon Dijon mustard
1   tablespoon fresh onion, minced
½   teaspoon salt
A few dashes pepper

Place bread cubes in a lightly oiled 1½ quart casserole dish. Sprinkle with one cup of cheddar cheese. In a medium bowl, combine eggs, milk, mustard, onion, salt and pepper. Pour over bread / cheese mixture. Top with remaining grated cheddar cheese. Refrigerate overnight. Allow casserole to come to room temperature before baking in a 350 oven for one hour, uncovered.

# SUMMERTIME TOMATO PIE

# Serves 4

I only prepare this dish when summer tomatoes are in season. You may use a frozen pie shell but for optimum flavor use the recipe for Flaky Pie Crust on page 143.

Complementing wine: a young Chianti

One 9-inch pie shell, baked according to directions
3-4  medium sliced tomatoes, (enough to nearly fill the pie shell)
½    cup mayonnaise
½    cup Parmesan cheese, divided
½    teaspoon dry mustard
½    teaspoon dried basil
¼    teaspoon cracked black pepper
½    teaspoon garlic powder
½    teaspoon salt
2    tablespoons fresh minced parsley

Preheat oven to 350. In a medium bowl, combine mayonnaise, ¼ cup Parmesan cheese, dry mustard, basil, black pepper, garlic powder, salt and parsley. Arrange tomatoes in the baked pie shell and evenly spread the mayonnaise mixture over tomatoes, sprinkle with the remaining Parmesan. Bake for 45 minutes or until lightly brown.

# GREEK SHRIMP SALAD

## Serves 4-6

Our friend, Jane Durkee, prepared this for my husband and me one glorious summer Sunday; it tasted as wonderful as the day was beautiful. The shrimp need to marinate in the dressing for 4 hours. Assemble the salad and the cut avocado just before serving. Delicious companions to this impressive meal are the Corn Muffins on page 137 or the rich and moist Chili Corn Bread on page 132.

Complementing wine: Pinot Grigio or Pinot Bianco

## DRESSING

¼　cup fresh lemon juice
½　teaspoon dried oregano
½　teaspoon dried basil
1　clove garlic, crushed
½　cup olive oil
½　cup fresh parsley, minced
½　teaspoon salt
Pepper to taste

## SALAD

2　pounds large shrimp, steamed, peeled and deveined
1　teaspoon canola oil
⅔　cup pecan halves
½　teaspoon dried oregano
½　cup green onions, thinly sliced
¾　cup Kalamata olives, pitted and chopped
4-6　servings of assorted lettuce leaves broken into bite size pieces
2-3　medium summer tomatoes cut into wedges
2　ripe Florida avocadoes cut into bite size cubes

Combine all dressing ingredients in a food processor and process until emulsified. Marinate shrimp in dressing for 4 hours. In a medium skillet, heat canola oil over moderate heat, sauté pecans and oregano until nuts are lightly browned. In a large bowl, toss green onions, olives and lettuce leaves, add to the marinated shrimp, and toss to combine. Divide salad among 4 serving plates. Arrange tomato wedges and avocado on top of salad. Garnish with toasted pecans.

# CREAMY CHICKEN AND ZUCCHINI

# CASSEROLE

## Serves 10

This dish is a great choice for a crowd and can be served for lunch, brunch or dinner. The Bloody Mary Aspic recipe on page 68 is a delicious accompaniment. I use the all-natural mushroom soup and stuffing mix, however any brand will work. This all around casserole can be prepared in advance and it doubles beautifully*

Complementing wine: Carneros Chardonnay

3    cooked chicken breasts, cut into bite size pieces
5-6  unpeeled medium zucchini, quartered and chopped into ½ inch
     pieces (about 4-5 cups)
Olive oil
1    large onion, finely chopped
1    large green pepper, chopped
1    can cream of mushroom soup
1    cup low fat sour cream
One 8-ounce bag herb stuffing mix
¼    cup butter (½ stick), melted
1    cup chicken broth
1    cup shredded sharp cheddar cheese

Preheat oven to 350. In a large pot, steam zucchini until tender-crisp, about 5 minutes. Remove from heat and transfer to a plate to cool. In a medium sauté pan, heat olive oil over moderate heat and sauté onion and green pepper until tender. In a large bowl, combine sautéed onion and green pepper with, zucchini, chicken, mushroom soup and sour cream. In a medium bowl, toss stuffing mix with melted butter and chicken broth. Line a 13x9-inch baking dish with stuffing mixture, reserving ½ cup for the top. Spoon zucchini mixture evenly over stuffing, top with grated cheese, finish with stuffing mixture, and bake uncovered for 1 hour.

\*    If you double this recipe, use 7-8 medium zucchini, 1 large and 1 small pepper and 3 medium onions, double the remaining ingredients.

# MARINATED SEA ISLAND SHRIMP

## Serves 10

The shrimp and dressing can be prepared in advance, toss the dish, however, just before serving. It is best to use summer tomatoes and sweet onions such as the Vidalia.

Complementing wine: California Riesling

5    pounds large or jumbo shrimp, steamed, peeled and deveined
4    medium ripe tomatoes, cubed
4    lemons, sliced
4    medium white onions cut into bite size chunks
½    teaspoon celery seed
2    teaspoons salt
1    teaspoon sugar
½    teaspoon black pepper
½    cup white wine vinegar
1    clove garlic, minced
1    teaspoon Worcestershire sauce
½    cup olive oil
½    cup canola oil

In a large bowl, gently toss shrimp, tomatoes, lemon slices and onion. In a medium bowl, combine celery seed, salt, sugar, pepper, vinegar, garlic and Worcestershire sauce. With a wire whisk, slowly add oil to vinegar mixture, whisk until well blended. Pour dressing over shrimp mixture just before serving.

# BEEF TENDERLOIN

# WITH BLUE CHEESE STUFFING

## Serves 4

This taste-treat tenderloin is among my husband's favorite recipes. Set the table with your favorite china and silver and light the candles.

Complementing wine: Napa Valley Cabernet Sauvignon or Left Bank Bordeaux

4   beef tenderloins (6-8 ounces each)
1   cup onion, chopped
4-6 slices of bacon cut into 1-inch pieces
⅓   cup sun-dried tomatoes, chopped
1   teaspoon dried rosemary, crushed
1   teaspoon dried basil
⅔   cup plain corn flakes, crushed
¾   cup blue cheese, crumbled

Preheat oven to 375. With a sharp knife, slice a horizontal pocket in each tenderloin. In a sauté pan over medium heat, cook the bacon and onion for about 5 minutes. Add sun-dried tomatoes and cook mixture until bacon and onion are lightly brown. Drain off all excess fat. Transfer bacon mixture to a medium bowl, add rosemary, basil, corn flakes and blue cheese. Toss until well combined. Pack about a ½ cup of stuffing into each tenderloin (some stuffing mixture will stick out) and bake for 5-7 minutes on each side or until desired doneness.

# BASIL SHRIMP PASTA

# Serves 6

I like the simplicity of this main dish entrée, most of it can be prepared in advance, toss with the dressing, however, just before serving.

Complementing wine: Pinot Grigio or Albarino

## DRESSING

3    cups fresh basil leaves
½    cup olive oil
¼    cup seasoned rice vinegar
Salt and pepper to taste

## PASTA

½    pound bow tie pasta cooked and cooled
1½   pounds large shrimp steamed, peeled and deveined
2    cups frozen peas, thawed
2    large ripe tomatoes cut into bite size pieces

Combine all dressing ingredients in a food processor and process until fully incorporated. In a large bowl, combine pasta, shrimp, peas and tomatoes. Toss pasta with dressing.

# BRISKET

## Serves 12

Liquid smoke gives this brisket its' distinct flavor, so bold is the flavor that I serve this brisket with plain steamed green beans and boiled new potatoes. The meat has to be cooked the day before you plan to serve it. Liquid smoke can be found in the condiment aisle of most grocery stores.

Complementing wine: Barossa Valley Shiraz or a full-bodied California Zinfandel

## BBQ SAUCE

2   cups catsup
2   cups water
2   teaspoons Worcestershire sauce
2   teaspoons liquid smoke
2   teaspoons brown sugar
1   teaspoon salt
A few dashes Tabasco sauce

## BRISKET

One 5 pound brisket, *after* the butcher has trimmed off all the fat
3-4 lemons, thinly sliced
3-4 medium onions, sliced

Preheat oven to 250. In a large bowl, combine all the ingredients for the BBQ sauce and refrigerate until ready to use. Place meat in a baking dish to accommodate and cover *first* with lemon slices and *second* with onion slices. Cover with tinfoil and bake for 6 hours. Drain liquid from meat and discard lemon and onion slices. Refrigerate overnight. The following day slice meat and cover with BBQ sauce. Bake Brisket in a 350 oven covered for 1 hour.

# MEDITERRANEAN SHRIMP

## Serves 6

A frisky tasting dish.

Complementing wine: Barbera di Asti or Cambrusco

¼  cup olive oil
4  cloves garlic, minced
1  red pepper, thinly sliced
2  pounds shrimp, peeled and deveined
One 26-ounce jar spicy red tomato sauce
One 15-ounce can artichoke hearts packed in water, drained, and
   quartered
One 8-ounce package spaghetti, Linguine or Angel Hair pasta,
   cooked according to package directions
½  cup feta cheese, crumbled

In a large skillet over medium heat, sauté garlic and red pepper in
olive oil, about 3 minutes, add shrimp and cook until shrimp are
opaque. Stir in red pepper sauce and artichokes. Simmer until tomato
sauce is bubbly. Spoon sauce over pasta and top with crumbled feta
cheese. Serve immediately.

# SEAFOOD LASAGNA

# Serves 6

It is best to prepare this one or two days in advance. The Brandied Carrots with Peas on page 56 and the Corn Chili Bread on page 132 are complimentary accompaniments to this dish.

Complementing wine: New Zealand Sauvignon Blanc or Chablis

## SHRIMP SOUP

3    tablespoons butter
1¼   cup onions, finely chopped
2    tablespoons flour
2    cups low fat or regular cow's milk
2    tablespoons crushed tomatoes
¼    pound cooked shrimp, diced
Pepper to taste
Cooking sherry to taste

In a skillet, melt butter over medium heat and sauté onion until translucent, whisk in flour. *Slowly* add milk, whisking constantly. Whisk until mixture becomes thick. Add tomatoes, shrimp, pepper and sherry; adjust seasonings.

## LASAGNA

⅔    box lasagna noodles, cooked according to package directions
1    pound lump crabmeat, picked of any shell
2    cups low fat cottage cheese
1    cup finely chopped onion
1    egg, lightly beaten
2    teaspoons salt
¼    teaspoon pepper

One 8-ounce package light cream cheese, softened
One 15-ounce can crushed tomatoes or 3-4 fresh sliced summer
    tomatoes
1    cup shredded white cheddar cheese

Preheat oven to 350. Fold crabmeat into shrimp soup. In a medium
bowl, combine cottage cheese, onion, egg, salt, pepper and cream
cheese. Spoon a layer of the shrimp mixture in the bottom of a 13x9
inch-baking dish, arrange a layer of lasagna noodles and cover
noodles with ½ of the cottage cheese mixture, repeat and cover with
tomatoes and shredded cheese. Cover and bake for 1 hour, remove
cover and bake an additional 15 minutes. Let stand 15 minutes before
serving.

# MARINATED BEEF TENDERLOIN

## Serves 25

This marinade is loaded with flavorful ingredients, resulting in a fork tender, tasty piece of beef, an impressive choice if you are planning a party. Plan accordingly, the tenderloin marinates for 24 hours.

Complementing wine: Red Bordeaux or Barolo

2    beef tenderloins (about 6 pounds each)

## MARINADE

1    cup pineapple juice
1    cup seasoned oil and vinegar dressing (whisk together 1 teaspoon salt, ground pepper to taste, ¼ cup apple cider vinegar, 1 teaspoon Dijon mustard and ¾ cup olive oil)
¾    teaspoon paprika
½    cup brown sugar
9    teaspoons celery seed
3    teaspoons black pepper
6    teaspoons dry mustard
6    teaspoons salt

## SAUCE

1    large onion, chopped
3    tablespoons rice vinegar
6    tablespoons brown sugar
⅓    cup Worcestershire sauce
3    cups ketchup

½    cup fresh lemon juice
3    teaspoons dry mustard
1½   teaspoons salt
1    teaspoon pepper

In a medium bowl, whisk together pineapple juice and dressing, pour over tenderloins. In a small bowl combine paprika, brown sugar, celery seed, pepper, dry mustard and salt. Sprinkle ½ of this mixture over the top of tenderloins. Marinate for 12 hours. Turn tenderloins and sprinkle remaining seasoning over the top of tenderloins, marinate for an additional 12 hours. In a large skillet over medium heat, sauté onion until light brown. Add vinegar, brown sugar, Worcestershire sauce, ketchup, lemon juice, dry mustard, salt and pepper, cook over medium low heat until thick, about ½ hour. Drain marinade and poor sauce over tenderloins. Remove meat for 2 hours before you bake in a 400 oven for: Rare: 35-40 minutes, medium rare: 45 minutes, medium: 50-60 minutes. Allow meat to stand 30 minutes or more before slicing.

# SESAME PORK TENDERLOIN WITH MUSTARD CREAM

## Serves 6

The amount of sesame seeds in this recipe is what makes this pork tenderloin unique and delicious. If you double the recipe, it is not necessary to double the sesame seeds. The Brandied Carrots and Peas, page 56, and the Creamy Mashed Potatoes, page 66 are delicious companions to this tenderloin. Place bowl and beaters in freezer for about 2 hours before preparing mustard cream recipe.

Complementing wine: Red Zinfandel

## MUSTARD CREAM

1   cup heavy whipping cream
1   tablespoon Worcestershire sauce
⅓   cup Dijon mustard, or more to taste

Pour cream into a medium bowl, beat on medium-high speed. When the cream thickens, lower the speed and continue to beat until cream falls in large globs and has soft peaks. Fold in Worcestershire sauce and mustard. Serve at room temperature.

## PORK

2   pork tenderloins (1 package)
½   cup light soy sauce or tamari
3   tablespoons sugar
2   tablespoons fresh minced onion
2   cloves garlic, minced
2   teaspoons ground ginger
¾   cup sesame seeds

In a baking dish to accommodate tenderloins, combine soy sauce or tamari, sugar, minced onion, garlic, ground ginger and sesame seeds. Add meat turning to coat on all sides. Marinate for 3 hours. Preheat oven to 375. Drain tenderloins and bake for 45 minutes.

# SHRIMP WITH LEMON AND GARLIC

## Serves 2-4

The rice in this recipe calls for fresh lemon peel, parsley and pepper, which further emphasizes the flavor of the shrimp. This company dish is good served with French bread and fresh steamed asparagus.

Complementing wine: Muscadet or White Bordeaux

1    cup uncooked texmati, basmati or jasmati rice
1¾  cups water
1    teaspoon salt
1    tablespoon fresh parsley
1    teaspoon lemon peel, finely grated
Pepper to taste
¼    cup butter
2    cloves garlic, minced
½    lemon thinly sliced
½    teaspoon oregano
1    bay leaf
½    teaspoon red pepper flakes*
½    teaspoon salt
1    pound shrimp, peeled and deveined**

In a medium saucepan, combine rice, water and salt, bring to a boil, cover, reduce heat and simmer for 15 minutes. Stir in parsley, lemon peel and pepper. Keep warm. In a sauté pan over moderate heat, melt butter and sauté garlic. Add lemon slices, oregano, bay leaf, red pepper flakes, salt and shrimp. Increase heat slightly, and sauté shrimp until cooked through, about 3-5 minutes. Discard bay leaf and spoon shrimp mixture over rice.

\*    If this seems too spicy, reduce amount to a ¼ teaspoon
\*\*  Frozen, steamed, peeled and deveined shrimp, thawed according to package directions works well in this recipe

# HOT SEAFOOD SALAD

# Serves 6

This is wonderful choice if you are planning a dinner party. For a colorful plate presentation, serve this entree alongside the Brandied Carrots with Peas on page 56 and the Seasoned Tomato Casserole on page 65. All three recipes can be prepared in advance, a hostess' dream!

Complementing wine: Sancerre, a dry Riesling, or a non-oaky white

1    pound jumbo lump crabmeat, picked of any shells
1    pound medium to large shrimp, steamed, peeled and deveined
1    small onion, finely chopped
½    cup celery, finely chopped
½    cup green pepper, finely chopped
1    cup mayonnaise
½    teaspoon salt
1    teaspoon Worcestershire sauce
⅛    teaspoon cracked black pepper
1    cup soft white bread (French or Italian) cut into small cubes
2    tablespoons melted butter

Preheat oven to 350. In a medium bowl, toss crab with shrimp. In a large bowl, combine onion, celery, green pepper, mayonnaise, salt, Worcestershire sauce and black pepper. Fold crab/shrimp mixture into mayonnaise. Spoon the seafood in an 8-inch baking dish. Toss bread cubes with melted butter and place over top of casserole. Bake for 25-30 minutes or until heated through.

# STUFFED CHICKEN BREASTS

## Serves 16

I like serving these chicken breasts for a seated dinner party along with steamed rice and the Brandied Carrots with Peas recipe on page 56. This recipe can be prepared early in the day you plan to serve it. The broth that comes from the cooked chicken is a tasty foundation for soup.

Complementing wine: California Chardonnay or Vouvray

8   whole chicken breasts cut in half (bone in, skin on)
2   tablespoons butter
2   medium onions, chopped
Two 10-ounce boxes frozen chopped spinach, thawed and squeezed
    dry
Two 15-ounce containers Ricotta cheese, regular or low fat
2   eggs, lightly beaten
½   cup chopped fresh parsley
½   teaspoon salt
¼   teaspoon nutmeg
Dijon mustard
Basil
Oregano
Paprika
Black pepper to taste

Preheat oven to 350. In a medium sauté pan over moderate heat, melt butter and sauté onion until translucent. Set aside. In a large bowl, combine spinach, Ricotta cheese, eggs, parsley, salt and nutmeg. Add onion and stir to combine all ingredients. Place chicken breasts in a single layer in a glass-baking dish. Gently lift the skin from each chicken breast and stuff with spinach mixture. Pull skin over chicken to cover breast. Spread each chicken breast evenly with Dijon mustard and *liberally* sprinkle the top of each breast with basil, oregano and paprika. Lightly season with black pepper. Bake for one hour uncovered. (If you double the recipe or if the chicken breasts are large, cook the breasts for an additional ½ hour—cover for the last hour.)

# SEAFOOD NEWBERG

## Serves 8-10

Choose any seafood combination for this recipe. Lobster and shrimp enhance one another and make for elegant dinner party fare. Serve Newberg over rice (recipe on page 93) that has been seasoned with lemon peel, minced fresh parsley and fresh ground pepper or spoon over toasted bread. Tasty accompaniments are fresh steamed asparagus topped with toasted slivered almonds and the Bloody Mary Aspic on page 68. Prepare Newberg at least one day in advance.

Complementing wine: Alsace such as a Pinot Blanc or a Riesling

2    cups low fat chicken broth
1    cup white wine
1    vegetable cube mixed with one cup boiling water
1    stick butter
1½   cups onion, finely chopped
⅔    cup white flour
7    cups cooked seafood (a half and half combination works well)
1    cup heavy cream
¼    cup cooking sherry
1    teaspoon salt
Black pepper to taste

In a medium pan, combine chicken broth, white wine, and vegetable cube mixture. Bring to a boil, reduce heat and simmer. In a large pan over moderate heat, melt butter and sauté onion until translucent. Whisk in flour ⅓ of a cup at a time and whisk until mixture comes together. Slowly add hot liquid combination whisking constantly. Whisk until mixture is well blended. Reduce heat to simmer, add seafood, cream, sherry, salt and pepper.

# Informal Main Dishes

Several recipes in this chapter have a higher nutritional value than those recipes in the Formal Main Dish Chapter. These recipes are great for mid-week meals, potluck parties, family gatherings or impromptu get-togethers. To make the meal complete, several recipes offer side dishes and all recipes offer a complementing beer or wine.

Tamale Pie
Spinach, Rice and Feta "Pie"
Curry Cashew Tuna Salad
Pasta with Pine Nuts
Chili Rellenos Casserole
Ginger Glazed Chicken
Vegetable Tagine with Harissa Sauce
Black Bean Enchiladas
Baked Tomatoes over Spinach and Lentils
Grilled Cheese and Caponata Sandwich
Superb Zucchini Casserole
Chili
Polenta Lasagna
Spinach Loaf
Pot Roast
Poached Eggs over Sauteed Shredded Wheat
Polenta with Roasted Peppers
Baked Ham

# TAMALE PIE

## Serves 6-8

While our nephew Travis was visiting one summer, I prepared this Mexican dish for dinner. My plan was to serve it for dinner and have the leftover for another meal. He ate the whole pie! I prepare this dish with fresh corn, frozen corn may be substituted with *almost* the same results.

Complementing wine: A soft, fruity red, perhaps a Beaujolais or a semi-sweet Riesling, a Spatlese for example

1¼  pounds lean ground chuck
2    teaspoons chili powder
One 16-ounce can condensed tomato soup
1    cup chopped peppers, any color
1    cup mild or medium salsa
½    cup water
1    recipe corn bread, recipe follows

In a medium skillet over moderate heat sauté ground chuck, add chili powder and cook until meat is brown, drain off any fat. Stir in tomato soup, peppers, salsa and water, bring to a boil, reduce heat to simmer and cook for about 5 minutes. Spoon mixture into a 13x9x2 inch-baking dish. Set aside.

## CORN BREAD

1½  cups fresh corn, or frozen
1    cup yellow cornmeal
2    teaspoons salt
3    teaspoons baking powder
1    cup low fat sour cream
⅓    cup olive oil

2     eggs, lightly beaten
¾     cup Monterey jack cheese, shredded
One 4-ounce can chopped green chilies, optional

Preheat oven to 350. In a large bowl, combine corn, cornmeal, salt, baking powder, sour cream, olive oil, eggs, cheese and chilies. Spoon mixture over tamale pie and bake for 45 minutes.

# SPINACH, RICE AND FETA "PIE"

## Serves 6

This dish is a good choice to have for a casual supper. Either the Red Cabbage Salad on page 50 or the Rainbow Salad on page 71 makes a delicious and colorful accompaniment.

Complementing wine: Greco di Tufo or Pinot Grigio

1    cup onion, chopped
Olive oil
1¼  cups cow's milk, any variety
¼   cup low fat sour cream
½   teaspoon salt
¼   teaspoon pepper
3    cups cooked rice, Basmati, Jasmati, or Texmati
¾   cup Valbresso feta cheese, crumbled
2    eggs, lightly beaten
One 16-ounce bag frozen chopped spinach thawed or 1 large bunch
     fresh cooked spinach chopped and thoroughly drained of excess
     liquid
3    tablespoons grated Parmesan cheese

Preheat oven to 400. Sauté onion in oil over medium heat until soft, transfer to a large bowl, and whisk in milk, sour cream, salt and pepper. Stir in rice, feta cheese, eggs and spinach, spoon into a 10-inch baking dish that has been coated with oil. Top mixture with Parmesan cheese. Bake for about 35-45 minutes or until light brown and bubbly.

# CURRY CASHEW TUNA SALAD

## Serves 4

For a simple luncheon or summer supper serve with sliced tomatoes, deviled eggs and a loaf of good quality French bread.

Complementing wine: Riesling, Spatlese or Auslese

2    cans solid white tuna packed in water, drained and flaked
⅓    cup raisins or dried cranberries
⅓    cup roasted cashews, chopped
2    tablespoons red, white or green onion, chopped
½    cup olive oil
¼    cup fresh lemon juice
1    clove garlic, minced
1    teaspoon curry powder
1    teaspoon fresh ginger, minced or ½ teaspoon dry
½    teaspoon salt
¼    teaspoon pepper
Lettuce leaves for garnish

In a medium bowl, toss tuna with raisins, cashews and onion. In a small bowl, combine olive oil, lemon juice, garlic, curry powder, ginger, salt and pepper, whisk until well blended. Just before serving, toss tuna with dressing. Garnish plates with lettuce leaves, top with tuna, serve immediately.

# PASTA WITH PINE NUTS

# Serves 4

Serve with a tossed green salad and slices of warm olive bread, (recipe on page 140).

Complementing wine: Valpolicella or Chianti Rufina

⅓   cup sun-dried tomatoes
1   cup boiling water
4   tablespoons olive oil
1   large onion, thinly sliced
4   cloves garlic, thinly sliced
2   tablespoons small capers
½   cup pine nuts, toasted
Salt and pepper to taste
1   pound linguine or angel hair pasta, cooked according to package directions
Fresh grated Parmesan cheese to taste

In a small bowl, combine sun-dried tomatoes with 1 cup boiling water and allow mixture to stand for 10-15 minutes. Remove tomatoes, reserving water, and cut into small pieces. In a sauté pan, heat oil over moderate heat, and sauté onion and garlic, cook until tender. Stir in tomato water, tomatoes, capers, pine nuts, salt and pepper. Divide pasta among 4 serving plates, spoon tomato mixture over hot cooked pasta, distributing evenly. Top with grated Parmesan cheese.

# CHILI RELLENOS CASSEROLE

## Serves 6

For an informal company dinner, plan a Mexican meal. Offer avocado Pate, (recipe on page 31) and salsa with tortilla chips as an appetizer. Steamed Swiss chard and Corn Muffins (recipe on page 137) are authentic accompaniments.

Complementing beverage: Sangria or a *true* Pilsner

½   pound lean ground chuck
1   cup onion, chopped
1½  teaspoons dried oregano
½   teaspoon garlic powder
¼   teaspoon salt
Fresh ground pepper to taste
One 16-ounce can refried beans
Two 4-ounce chopped green chilies, divided
1   cup shredded Monterey Jack cheese, divided use
1   cup fresh or frozen corn
⅓   cup flour
¼   teaspoon salt
1⅓  cups cow's milk, any variety
⅛   teaspoon Tabasco or hot pepper sauce
3   eggs, lightly beaten
Salsa and low fat sour cream accompaniments

Preheat oven to 350. In a large skillet over medium heat, cook ground chuck and onion until brown. Drain off any excess fat, stir in oregano, garlic powder, salt, pepper and refried beans. Line the bottom of an 11x7 inch-baking dish, with one can of the chopped green chilies. Top with ½ cup of the cheese and spoon beef/bean mixture over cheese, leaving a ¼ inch border around the edge of dish. Distribute corn and remaining green chilies over beef and bean mixture, top with cheese. In a medium bowl, combine flour and salt, whisk in milk, Tabasco or hot sauce and eggs, pour over casserole and bake uncovered for 1 hour.

# GINGER GLAZED CHICKEN

## Serves 4

A simple chicken dish that can be grilled or baked.

¼   cup Dijon mustard
2   tablespoons brown sugar
2   tablespoons honey
1   tablespoon minced fresh ginger
4   chicken cutlets, about 1¼ pounds

Preheat oven to 375 or prepare grill. In a medium bowl, combine mustard, brown sugar, honey and ginger. Place cutlets in a lightly oiled 11x7-inch baking dish and brush both sides of chicken with mustard mixture. Bake for 15 minutes on each side. Set oven temperature to broil and broil for 1-2 minutes on each side or until golden and slightly blackened. To grill, place chicken on rack and brush with half the mustard mixture, grill for 5 minutes. Turn chicken and brush with remaining mustard mixture, grill for an additional 5 minutes or until chicken is cooked through.

# VEGETABLE TAGINE WITH HARISSA SAUCE

## Serves 6

The harissa sauce is very hot but I think it compliments the vegetable tagine perfectly, use it sparingly until you know its aftereffects. The leftover harissa sauce (which keeps for weeks in the refrigerator) is a striking companion to sautéed tofu. If you have any Vegetable Tagine leftover, add a can of chicken broth, 1 cup of chopped tomatoes and 1 cup frozen spinach, the result is a tasty pot of soup!

Complementing wine: Sauvignon Blanc or a New Zealand Riesling

2 tablespoons olive oil
1 large onion, chopped
1 red pepper chopped into ½ inch dice
1 yellow pepper cut into ½ inch dice
2 cans artichoke hearts drained and quartered
2 cans chickpeas with liquid, divided use
¾ cup pitted Kalamata olives, chopped
1 tablespoon lemon peel, grated
1 teaspoon fresh lemon juice
3 tablespoons minced parsley
1 box of couscous with pine nuts cooked according to package directions

Preheat oven to 350. In a medium skillet, heat oil over moderate heat and sauté onion and red and yellow peppers until tender. Remove from heat, add, artichokes, one can of chickpeas, olives, lemon peel, lemon juice, and parsley. Stir well to distribute ingredients evenly. Set aside. Combine remaining can of chickpeas with the cooked couscous. Spoon couscous mixture into a 13x9x2 inch baking dish, top with vegetable mixture and bake for 30-40 minutes or until heated through.

# HARISSA SAUCE

½   cup olive oil
1   teaspoon cayenne pepper
2   tablespoons tomato paste
¼   cup fresh lime juice (about 1 medium lime)
½   teaspoon salt

In a small bowl, combine olive oil, cayenne pepper, tomato paste, lime juice and salt, whisk until mixture is emulsified. The olive oil will naturally separate from the remaining ingredients, stir or whisk just before serving.

# BLACK BEAN ENCHILADAS

# Serves 6

Compliment this dish with the Mango and Cashew Salad with Lime Dressing on page 64.

Complementing wine: a soft, fruity red such as a Shiraz or Zinfandel

Olive oil
1   cup onion, chopped
1   tablespoon garlic, minced
2   teaspoons chili powder
2   teaspoons cumin powder
¼   teaspoon oregano
¼   teaspoon salt
⅛   teaspoon ground red pepper
One 14-ounce can chopped tomatoes with juice
Two 15-ounce cans black beans, drained
One 4-ounce can chopped green chilies
2   cups shredded Monterey Jack cheese, divided
Six 7-inch soft flour tortillas
¼   cup chopped green onions, for garnish

Preheat oven to 350. In a large skillet over medium heat, heat oil and sauté onion and garlic, stir in chili powder, cumin, oregano, salt and red pepper, sauté for one minute, stir in tomatoes. Transfer 1 cup of tomato mixture to a small bowl. Add black beans and green chilies to the tomato mixture in the sauté pan. Sprinkle about ¼ cup cheese down the center of one tortilla shell and top with about ½ cup black bean mixture. Roll tortilla shell and place seam side down into a 13x9-inch baking dish. Repeat with remaining tortilla shells. Spoon reserved tomato mixture over enchiladas, sprinkle with remaining cheese and bake for 45 minutes or until bubbly. Garnish with chopped green onions.

# BAKED TOMATOES OVER SPINACH

# AND LENTILS

## Serves 4

I use summer tomatoes and fresh spinach for this recipe. The combination is delicious and so fresh tasting that I did not bother testing canned tomatoes or frozen spinach. For a complete meal, I serve this with scrambled eggs to which I have folded in cream cheese.

Complementing wine: Salice Salentino or Rosso di Montepulciano

4     medium tomatoes cored and cut in half width wise
1     teaspoon dried basil
2     cloves garlic, minced
2     teaspoons olive oil
Salt and pepper to taste
1     bunch fresh spinach, thoroughly washed
1     teaspoon salt
1     cup red lentils, rinsed

## SCRAMBLED EGGS

8     eggs lightly beaten
3-4  tablespoons light cream cheese, softened

Preheat oven to 400. Sprinkle tomatoes with basil, garlic, olive oil, salt and pepper. Bake for one hour. Place spinach in a large pot, set aside. In a large pot, bring 4 cups of water to a boil, add 1 teaspoon salt and lentils, cook for 30-40 minutes or until tender. Shortly before the tomatoes have finished their cooking time, steam spinach for 3-4 minutes or until wilted. Divide lentils among 4 serving bowls, top with spinach and 2 tomato halves. If desired, serve with scrambled eggs laced with cream cheese. Serve immediately.

# GRILLED CHEESE
# AND CAPONATA SANDWICH

I've taken the ordinary toasted cheese sandwich and added caponata (recipe on page 32). Select your favorite bread for grilling as well as your favorite cheese to use in this recipe.

Complementing wine: Saint Veran

Sliced bread
Sliced cheese
Caponata
Better butter (recipe on page 142)

Butter bread and place sliced cheese on unbuttered side of bread. Spoon a desired amount of caponata over cheese, top caponata with another slice of cheese, top with remaining slice of buttered bread. In a medium skillet, over moderately high heat, grill sandwich for about 2-3 minutes on each side or until bread is light brown and the cheese has melted. Serve immediately.

# SUPERB ZUCCHINI CASSEROLE

# Serves 6

This is a good summer dish to prepare when zucchini's harvest is at its' peak. You may prepare this early the day that you plan to serve it, bake it however just before serving. It is delicious with the Bloody Mary Aspic on page 68 and a crusty loaf of bread.

Complementing wine: Orvieto Classico

| | |
|---|---|
| 2 | medium zucchini (1 pound) unpeeled and cut into cubes |
| 1 | medium onion (about ½ cup) diced |
| ½ | teaspoon salt |
| ¼ | teaspoon black pepper |
| ½ | teaspoon dried oregano |
| ½ | teaspoon dried thyme |
| ½ | teaspoon dry mustard |
| 6 | eggs, beaten |
| 2 | cups grated low-fat Swiss cheese or cheddar cheese, divided use |

Preheat the oven to 325. In a medium pot, steam zucchini and onion until *just tender*, gently mash zucchini. In a small bowl, combine salt, pepper, oregano, thyme and mustard, set aside. In a large bowl, combine eggs and 1½ cups of cheese, whisk in spices, add onion and zucchini and pour into a greased 1½ quart baking dish. Top with remaining ½ cup of cheese. Bake for 45-50 minutes or until light brown.

# CHILI

## Serves 4-6

I like the ingredient proportions in this chili recipe. With little preparation and lots of flavor, this chili is ready in just one hour. Serve it with a tossed salad and either the Corn Chili Bread (page 132) or the Corn Muffins (page 137). Tortilla chips are also useful and fun for dipping the chili from your bowl. If desired, top each bowl with a dollop of sour cream, shredded cheddar cheese and chopped raw onion.

Complementing wine: medium-bodied Zinfandel or Sangria

1    pound lean ground chuck
1    medium onion, chopped
1    tablespoon chili powder
1    tablespoon Old Bay seasoning
¼    teaspoon garlic powder
1    teaspoon Worcestershire sauce
2    cups tomato sauce
Two 15-ounce cans kidney beans, drained
One 16-ounce can whole tomatoes

In a large pot, over moderate heat cook the ground chuck, and drain off liquid. Add the onion and sauté until tender. Stir in the chili powder, Old Bay seasoning, garlic powder, Worcestershire sauce, tomato sauce, kidney beans and tomatoes; combine well. Cover, bring to a boil, reduce heat to medium–low and cook for 1 hour.

# POLENTA LASAGNA

## Serves 4

This dish is attractive, nutritious and simple to prepare.

Complementing wine: Valtelino Red or Valpolicello

1¼  cups low fat ricotta cheese
½    teaspoon crushed red pepper
1    teaspoon dried basil
Salt and pepper to taste
1    bunch fresh spinach, steamed, chopped and drained of any
     liquid or 1 box frozen chopped spinach, thawed and drained of
     any liquid
½    cup Parmesan cheese, divided use
One 16-ounce tube polenta cut into 16 slices
1    cup marinara sauce

Preheat oven to 350. In a medium bowl, combine ricotta cheese, red
pepper, basil, salt, pepper, spinach and ¼ cup Parmesan cheese.
Coat a 13x9-inch baking dish with cooking spray. Arrange eight of
the polenta slices in the bottom of baking dish, spoon ½ of the ricotta/
spinach mixture over the polenta and top with ½ cup of the marinara
sauce. Repeat with the polenta, ricotta/spinach and marinara sauce,
top with ¼ cup Parmesan cheese, cover and bake for 30 minutes.
Remove cover, place oven temperature to broil to allow top to brown.

# SPINACH LOAF

# Serves 4

Serve this hearty, nutritious loaf with either sliced summer tomatoes, the Orange Marmalade Tomatoes on page 53 or the Seasoned Tomato Casserole on page 65.

Complementing wine: Sauvignon Blanc or a semi-dry Riesling

2    tablespoons better butter, recipe on page 142
1    large onion, chopped
3    cloves garlic, minced
½    pound mushrooms, chopped
1    bunch fresh spinach washed, steamed, chopped and drained of excess water or one 16-ounce package chopped frozen spinach, thawed, and drained of any liquid
½    cup chicken or vegetable broth
2    tablespoons parsley, minced
½    teaspoon ground cumin
2    teaspoons dried oregano
1½  tablespoons soy sauce or tamari
1    cup ground almonds
1    cup breadcrumbs
½    cup wheat germ
2    eggs, lightly beaten

Preheat oven to 350. In a skillet over moderate heat, melt better butter and sauté onion, garlic and mushrooms until soft. Remove from heat and stir in spinach, broth, parsley, ground cumin, oregano and tamari. In a large bowl, combine almonds, breadcrumbs and wheat germ, whisk in eggs, add mushroom/broth mixture and combine well. Shape into a loaf and place in a lightly oiled baking dish, bake for 30 minutes or until brown.

# POT ROAST

## Serves 6

Feel free to use any combination of vegetables you like to cook with this roast. Freshly grated horseradish or prepared horseradish is a delicious accompaniment to the roast. Leftover essence can be used as a stock for soup.

Complementing wine: Russian River Pinot Noir

One 4-pound beef chuck roast, trimmed of fat
1     garlic clove, crushed
White flour
Canola oil
1     teaspoon salt
½     teaspoon pepper
2-3  medium onions, quartered
2     cans (14.25 ounce) chicken broth
4     medium tomatoes
4-6  small to medium red potatoes, quartered
6-8  carrots cut 2-3 inches long on the diagonal
3     small turnips, peeled and quartered
4     parsnips, peeled cut 2-3 inches long on the diagonal
3-4  stalks celery cut 4-5 inches long

Preheat oven to 325. Rub roast with garlic and dredge in flour, coating all sides. In a large skillet, heat oil to medium high and brown meat on all sides, remove meat, season with salt and pepper. Place meat, onions and chicken broth in a roasting pan to accommodate and cook for 1 hour. Add vegetables and cook for another 2-3 hours. Turn vegetables once or twice to assure even cooking. Arrange pot roast on platter and surround with vegetables. Serve immediately.

# POACHED EGGS OVER SAUTÉED

# SHREDDED WHEAT

## Serves 4

I like the combination of the salty, crunchy, buttery shredded wheat with the soft poached egg, and the texture is magnificent. Serve for breakfast or brunch.

Complementing beverage: Mimosa

1   tablespoon apple cider vinegar
2   tablespoons better butter (recipe on page 142)
4   shredded wheat biscuits, crumbled
4   eggs
Salt and pepper to taste

Fill a 2-quart pot with 1½ quarts of water stir in apple cider vinegar. Bring water to a boil and reduce heat to medium (water should rumble). In a medium skillet, over moderate heat, melt butter, add crumbled shredded wheat and sauté until crispy, season with salt to taste. Set aside. Break egg into a small cup and gently slide egg into water, working quickly repeat with remaining eggs. Cook eggs 3-5 minutes. Whites should be firm and yokes soft. While eggs are cooking, divide shredded wheat among four serving plates. Remove eggs with a slotted spoon, drain of any excess water and place egg on top of shredded wheat, season with salt and pepper.

# POLENTA WITH ROASTED PEPPERS

## Serves 6

A robust dish with lots of flavor and color. To further enhance its color presentation, serve with either, The Red Cabbage Salad on page 50 or the Rainbow Salad on page 71.

Complementing wine: Bardolino or Dolletto

3      large peppers, any color
One 14-ounce can tomatoes, chopped
One 16-ounce tube polenta, sliced
1¼   cups shredded Fontina cheese
Fresh basil

Preheat broiler. Cut peppers in half remove stems and seeds. Place pepper halves skin side up on a baking sheet and flatten them with the palm of your hand. Broil peppers for 10 minutes or until blackened. Remove from oven and place peppers in a plastic bag, seal bag and let stand for 15 minutes. Reduce oven temperature to 350. Pull skin from peppers and cut into strips. In a medium bowl, combine peppers and tomatoes. Spoon ½ of the tomato/pepper mixture into a 13x9-inch baking dish and top with ½ the polenta. Repeat with the tomato/pepper mixture and polenta, top dish with cheese and bake for 25 minutes. Broil for 1-2 minutes to brown top.

# BAKED HAM

# 1 Ham

If planning a casual or family supper, complimentary accompaniments are the Marinated Potato Salad, page 58, Green Beans and Spiced Walnuts with Feta, page 52, and the Honey-Curry Glazed Pineapple in the Miscellany section. This ham is tasty as well with the Sweet Potato Biscuits, page 129.

Complementing wine: Riesling or Gewurztraminer

1   butt end ham
1   cup chicken broth
1   cup white wine
2   stalks celery, cut into large chunks
2   medium carrots, peeled and cut into large chunks
2   medium onions, quartered

Preheat oven to 350. Place ham in a roasting pan and add chicken broth, wine, celery, carrots and onions. Cover roasting pan and bake for 1½-2 hours. Remove ham from roasting pan and discard celery, carrots and onions. Allow ham to cool slightly before carving. Leftover broth makes a delicious soup. To skim fat from broth refrigerate overnight.

# Breads and Baked Goods

If you have not made homemade bread and the thought of the endeavor intimidates you, try to revisit bread baking. I remember with fondness coming home from school to the smell of homemade bread baking in the oven, a memory that lingers with me today. However wonderful the memory and aroma, I did not set out to make a loaf until I was in my late thirties. In Tips, Alternatives and Suggestions, I offer a brief "guide" on bread making tips.

Delicious Biscuits
Flaxseed Bread
Muffins with Black Olives
Goat Cheese and Olive Stuffed Bread
Corn Cakes
Hearty Pancakes
Muffins with Molasses and Bran
Sweet Potato Biscuits
Muenster Cheese Bread
Parsnip Pancakes
Corn Chili Bread
Jam and Cream Cheese Log
Butternut Squash Bread
Zucchini Pancakes
Green Onion Won Ton Rounds
Corn Muffins
Oven Baked Pancake
Hearty Whole Wheat Bread
Olive Bread

# DELICIOUS BISCUITS

## 2 Dozen Biscuits

A tasty biscuit that makes a nice accompaniment to soups and salads.

1   package active dry yeast
½   cup warm water
4   cups white flour
½   cup raw wheat germ
½   cup wheat flour
¼   cup plus 1 teaspoon sugar
1   teaspoon baking powder
1   teaspoon baking soda
1   teaspoon salt
½   cup canola oil
2   cups low fat buttermilk

In a medium bowl, combine the yeast and 1 teaspoon sugar. Add warm water and stir until mixture is dissolved; allow to proof about 5 minutes. In a large mixing bowl combine white flour, wheat germ, wheat flour, ¼ cup sugar, baking powder, baking soda and salt. Slowly drizzle oil over flour mixture, "toss" with a fork until mixture resembles coarse meal. Add yeast mixture and buttermilk stir until moist. Cover and chill for 1 hour or overnight.

Preheat oven to 450. Turn dough out onto a heavily floured surface and knead several times. Roll into a ½ inch thickness and cut with a 3-inch biscuit cutter. Arrange biscuits on a greased baking sheet and bake for 11-13 minutes or until golden.

# FLAXSEED BREAD .

# 2 Loaves

Flaxseeds and wheat germ make this a nutritious loaf that is a good keeper and makes the most memorable toast.

½   cup cornmeal
1   cup boiling water
1   teaspoon salt
2   packages active dry yeast
1   tablespoon sugar
½   cup warm water
1   cup warm milk, any variety except buttermilk
2   teaspoons salt
¼   cup light brown sugar
½   cup flaxseeds
½   cup raw wheat germ
3-4  cups white flour

Pour cornmeal into 1 cup boiling salted water and stir vigorously until mixture is thick, about 2 minutes. Allow mixture to cool. In a large mixing bowl, proof the yeast with the sugar in the ½ cup warm water, add cooled cornmeal mixture and stir well to combine. Add the warm milk, salt, brown sugar, flaxseeds and wheat germ. Add flour 1 cup at a time, stirring well after each addition. When the dough begins to pull away from the sides of the bowl turn out to a floured board and knead dough for about 10 minutes adding more flour as necessary to keep from sticking. Dough should be smooth and elastic. Place dough in a large bowl that has been coated with cooking spray, cover and allow to rise in a warm draft free spot until double in bulk. Punch dough down, cut in half and shape into two loaves, place in 9x5x3-inch bread pans that have coated with cooking spray, cover and allow to rise until double in bulk about 1 hour. Bake in a 425 oven for 10 minutes, reduce heat to 350 and bake an additional

20-25 minutes or until bread is light brown and sounds hollow when you tap the bottom. Place the loaves without tins on the oven rack and bake for 1-2 minutes, to crisp the crust. Cool on racks before slicing.

# MUFFINS WITH BLACK OLIVES

# 10 Muffins

The addition of Kalamata olives makes these muffins moist. A nice compliment to the Grilled Hamburger Soup on page 38.

1½  cups white flour
½   cup raw wheat germ
2½  teaspoons baking powder
½   teaspoon salt, optional
1   cup milk, any variety
3   tablespoons olive oil
1   egg, lightly beaten
1   cup chopped black olives, preferably Kalamata olives

Preheat oven to 400. In a large bowl, combine white flour, wheat germ, baking powder and salt. In a small bowl, whisk together milk, olive oil and egg. Make a well in the center of the flour mixture; add the milk mixture and stir just to combine. Fold in chopped olives, distribute evenly. Spoon muffin mixture into greased muffin cups, and bake for 15 minutes or until toothpick inserted in the center comes out clean.

# GOAT CHEESE

# AND OLIVE STUFFED BREAD

## One medium loaf

A filled loaf that is delicious served with soup or a hearty salad. This dough is easy to work with.

| | |
|---|---|
| 2 | packages active dry yeast |
| 1 | teaspoon sugar |
| 1 | cup warm water |
| 2 | cups white flour |
| ¼ | cup raw wheat germ |
| 1 | teaspoon salt |
| ½ | cup seasoned Goat cheese spread |
| ¾ | cup chopped Kalamata black olives |
| 1 | egg white |

In a large bowl, combine yeast and sugar, add warm water, and let stand in a warm place until foamy. In a medium bowl, combine, flour, wheat germ and salt; add yeast mixture and stir until well blended. Knead the dough and gradually add more flour; knead for about 5 minutes until you have a smooth, elastic dough. Place dough in a large bowl that has been coated with cooking spray. Cover and allow to rise in a warm, draft free spot for about 45 minutes to 1 hour. Punch dough down and roll out onto a floured surface into an 11x7-inch rectangle. Spread with Goat cheese and sprinkle with olives leaving a one-inch border. Roll into a log, pinch edges to seal and tuck ends under. With a sharp knife, make several slits across the top of the loaf. Place loaf on an oiled baking sheet, cover and let rest for about 45 minutes. Brush loaf with egg white and bake in a 375 oven for 30 minutes or until golden brown. Let stand for 10 minutes before slicing.

# CORN CAKES

## About fourteen 4-inch pancakes

Fresh corn is abundant in the summer and it seems I am always gratefully de-cobbing! I often serve these cakes with soup and a salad and sometimes for breakfast.

2    cups fresh corn (frozen if fresh is not available)
2    eggs, lightly beaten
2    tablespoons olive oil
½    cup yellow cornmeal
1    cup milk, any variety
½    cup white flour
1    teaspoon baking powder
¼    teaspoon salt
¼    cup sun-dried tomato bits, optional

In a food processor, combine corn, eggs and olive oil, pulse until combined. Add cornmeal and milk, pulse until blended. Add flour, baking powder and salt. In a medium skillet, heat oil over moderately high heat and drop batter by the tablespoon and cook for about 2 minutes on each side. Serve immediately.

# HEARTY PANCAKES

## Serves 8

A Teflon pan works well to cook these pancakes, but if you use a cast iron skillet, generously oil the pan.

1¼ cups water
½ teaspoon salt
½ cup yellow cornmeal
½ cup quick cooking oatmeal
1 egg, lightly beaten
2 tablespoons canola oil or olive oil, plus extra for frying
1¼ cups milk, any variety* (soy milk works well)
¼ cup wheat germ
¼ cup whole-wheat flour
⅛ cup millet, toasted
⅛ cup flaxseeds
1 tablespoon bran flakes, optional
2 teaspoons baking powder

In a medium saucepan, bring water and salt to a boil; slowly stir in cornmeal and oatmeal. Stir vigorously, reduce heat to low and simmer until very thick, about 3-5 minutes. Allow mixture to cool. In a large bowl, combine egg, oil and milk. Add cornmeal mixture and stir until well combined. In a small bowl, combine wheat germ, whole-wheat flour, millet, flaxseeds, bran flakes and baking powder. Add to the cornmeal/milk mixture and stir until fully combined. In a large skillet, heat oil over moderately high heat, spoon batter into skillet and fry until golden brown on each side about 1-2 minutes.

* As this mixture settles it thickens, add additional milk for desired consistency.

# MUFFINS WITH MOLASSES AND BRAN

## 8 Large Muffins

My 16-year-old nephew eats one batch of these muffins in one sitting! This recipe doubles beautifully.

3    tablespoons canola oil
2    tablespoons honey
2    tablespoons molasses
1    egg, lightly beaten
1½  cups milk, any variety (low-fat buttermilk or soy milk makes a richer muffin)
1    cup whole-wheat flour
1½  cups bran
½    teaspoon salt
1    teaspoon baking soda
½    cup flaxseeds, optional

Preheat oven to 375. In a large mixing bowl, whisk together oil, honey, molasses, egg and milk. In a medium bowl, combine whole-wheat flour, bran, salt, baking soda and flaxseeds. Stir into milk mixture. Pour bran mixture into 8 greased or paper-lined muffin cups filling them just to the top and bake for 17-20 minutes or until toothpick inserted in center of muffins comes out clean.

# SWEET POTATO BISCUITS

## 16 Biscuits

A moist, sweet and colorful biscuit that is delicious with a hearty bowl of soup and/or slices of Baked Ham, recipe on page 119.

2    cups white flour
⅓    cup yellow cornmeal
2½   teaspoons baking powder
½    teaspoon salt
⅓    cup olive oil
1    cup cooked sweet potato, mashed (one large)
½    cup milk, any variety
2    tablespoons honey

Preheat oven to 400. In a large bowl, combine flour, cornmeal, baking powder and salt. Drizzle oil over flour mixture and using a fork, "toss" flour, allowing flour to absorb oil. Add sweet potato, milk and honey. Knead dough (dough will be sticky) until well combined. Sprinkle work surface with flour, form dough into a "rough" 9-inch square, cut into 16 squares. Place on a greased baking sheet and bake for 20 minutes or until golden brown.

# MUENSTER CHEESE BREAD

## 1 loaf

I like to serve this with a bowl of the Grilled Hamburger Soup on page 38.

| | |
|---|---|
| 2 | packages active dry yeast |
| 1 | teaspoons sugar |
| 1 | cup warm water |
| ¼ | cup olive oil |
| 2 | teaspoons salt |
| 2-3 | cups white flour |
| 4 | cups (1 pound) shredded Muenster cheese |
| 1 | egg white, lightly beaten |

In a large mixing bowl, combine yeast and sugar; dissolve with warm water. Allow mixture to proof for about 5 minutes. Stir in olive oil, salt and 2 cups of flour, stir until smooth. Add enough of the remaining flour to make a soft dough, turn out to a floured board and knead for about 6-8 minutes adding more flour if necessary. Knead until you have a smooth, elastic dough. Place dough in large oiled bowl, cover with a kitchen towel and allow to rise in a warm draft free spot until doubled in bulk, about 1 hour. Punch dough down and roll into a 16-inch diameter. Place dough in an oiled 9-inch round cake pan; allow the dough to drape over the sides of the pan. Spoon the grated cheese into the center of the dough. Gather dough up over filling in 1½ inch pleats. Gently squeeze pleats together at top and twist dough to make a top "knot." Cover and allow loaf to rise in a warm spot free of drafts for 30 minutes. Brush loaf with lightly beaten egg white if desired and bake in a 375 oven for 45 minutes. Serve warm.

# PARSNIP PANCAKES

## Yields 14 pancakes

I have served these delicious morsels as an appetizer, as an accompaniment to soup, at breakfast (with fresh fruit) and as an informal dessert. They are *always* well received. Spread good quality ginger marmalade over them.

1   egg, lightly beaten
2   tablespoons buttermilk or any variety of milk
½   cup white flour
1   teaspoon baking powder
½   teaspoon salt
Dash pepper
2   medium parsnips, peeled and grated in a food processor (2 cups)
Olive oil
Ginger Marmalade

In a medium bowl, combine egg and milk. Stir in flour, baking powder, salt and pepper. Fold in parsnips. Let batter rest for 15-30 minutes. In a medium skillet, heat olive oil over moderate heat, drop tablespoons of batter into skillet and cook until brown on both sides, about 2 minutes on each side. Repeat until you have cooked all the pancakes. Serve immediately with ginger marmalade if desired.

# CORN CHILI BREAD

# Serves 8

A moist and rich bread that compliments Mexican fare, soups, salads and casseroles. For elegant dinner fare, serve with the Seafood Lasagna on page 87.

1    cup yellow cornmeal
2    teaspoons salt
3    teaspoons baking powder
1½  cups fresh corn
1    cup low fat sour cream
⅓   cup olive oil
2    eggs, lightly beaten
¾   cup grated Monterey Jack cheese
One 4-ounce can chopped green chilies

Preheat oven to 350. In a small bowl, combine cornmeal, salt and baking powder. In a large bowl, mix until well blended the corn, sour cream, oil, eggs, cheese and green chilies. Add flour mixture to wet ingredients and stir to combine. Pour batter into a greased 10-inch baking dish and bake for 1 hour.

# JAM AND CREAM CHEESE LOG

# 1 large loaf

This bread is a good choice if you are planning a brunch. Complimentary accompaniments are scrambled eggs served with sausage or bacon. The loaf must be prepared the day before you plan to serve it.

1    package active dry yeast
1    tablespoon sugar
⅛    cup water
2¼   cups white flour
¼    cup wheat germ
1    teaspoon baking powder
1    teaspoon baking soda
½    teaspoon salt
1    egg, lightly beaten
½    cup raspberry preserves or your favorite preserves
One 8-ounce package light cream cheese

In a large bowl, dissolve yeast and sugar with warm water, let stand in a warm place until foamy. In a medium bowl, combine flour, wheat germ, baking powder, baking soda and salt; combine with yeast mixture. Add egg and mix well. Knead dough several times and place dough in the center of a greased baking sheet. Roll dough into a 14x9-inch rectangle. In a small bowl, combine preserves with cream cheese, spread mixture down the center of the rectangle, roll dough into a log. With a sharp knife, make 3-inch long slits at 1-inch intervals. Cover dough loosely with plastic wrap, refrigerate overnight. Allow dough to come to room temperature before baking in a 350 oven for 25-30 minutes.

# BUTTERNUT SQUASH BREAD

## 2 loaves

This is a lovely loaf with a beautiful buttery color. The flavor is like squash itself—mellow. It is delicious just from the oven, but it also makes a memorable piece of toast. Either way it is a tasty loaf to use for sandwiches or as an accompaniment with soup.

| | |
|---|---|
| 2 | packages active dry yeast |
| ½ | cup warm water |
| 1 | teaspoon sugar |
| 1¼ | cups cooked butternut squash, mashed |
| 1 | cup warm milk, any variety |
| 2 | tablespoons olive oil |
| 1¼ | cups brown sugar |
| 3 | teaspoons salt |
| 1 | cup raw wheat germ |
| 5-6 | cups white flour |

In a large bowl, combine yeast with the warm water and 1 teaspoon sugar, allow mixture to proof. When yeast mixture is foamy stir in squash, milk, olive oil, brown sugar, salt and wheat germ. Add flour one cup at a time, when dough begins to pull away from the sides of the bowl, transfer to a floured surface. Knead until dough is smooth and elastic, about 10 minutes. Place dough in a large bowl that has been coated with cooking spray, turn dough to oil the surface, cover and let rise in a warm draft free spot until doubled in bulk, about 1 hour. Punch dough down and divide into 2 loaves and place in a greased 9x5x2-inch loaf pans, cover and let rise until doubled, about ½ hour. Bake loaves in a 375 oven for 25-30 minutes or until golden brown. Remove loaves from pans and cool on wire rack before serving.

# ZUCCHINI PANCAKES

## Yields 14 pancakes

Pesto sauce, (recipe on page 154) is a delicious dip for these vegetable pancakes. If you have a counter service style kitchen where your guests can be with you while you cook the pancakes, this is a good choice to serve for an appetizer. They likely will eat them faster than you can cook them!

1    egg, lightly beaten
2    tablespoons buttermilk
½    cup white flour
1    teaspoon baking powder
½    teaspoon salt
Pepper to taste
A few dashes Tabasco or hot pepper sauce
2    cups unpeeled zucchini, grated in a food processor
½    cup onion, minced
Olive oil

In a medium bowl, combine egg and milk. Stir in flour, baking powder, salt, pepper and Tabasco or hot sauce. Fold in zucchini and onion. Let batter rest for 15-30 minutes. In a medium skillet, heat olive oil over medium high heat; drop tablespoons of batter into skillet and cook until brown on both sides about 2 minutes on each side. Repeat until you have cooked all the pancakes. Serve immediately with pesto sauce.

# GREEN ONION WON TON ROUNDS

## 6 thin pancakes

These remind me of an appetizer that a neighborhood Chinese restaurant served many years ago. Dip into the Sesame Ginger dressing recipe on page 150.

1⅛  cups white flour
¼   cup wheat germ
½   cup scallions, thinly sliced, green part only
½   teaspoon salt
½   cup water
Olive oil for cooking

In a medium bowl, combine flour, wheat germ, scallions and salt. Add water and stir to combine. Knead dough for a few minutes adding more flour if necessary to keep dough from sticking. Divide dough into 6 equal pieces. Roll each piece on a floured surface into a thin circle and set aside. To keep pancakes from sticking to one another use plastic wrap between each pancake. In a large skillet over medium high heat, heat oil and cook won ton rounds one at a time until brown on each side, about 1-2 minutes. Cool slightly before cutting into wedges.

# CORN MUFFINS

# 10 large muffins

I have experimented, with various additions to these easy, delicious muffins. Dried cranberries, sun-dried tomatoes, flaxseeds, scallions and peanuts are all delicious choices. One of my favorite additions however, is to place a ½ teaspoon hot pepper jam in the middle of each muffin before baking. If you do not want the individualistic muffins, bake the batter in a cake pan and cut into wedges.

1    cup white flour
¾   cup yellow cornmeal
¼   cup wheat germ
3    tablespoons sugar, optional
5    teaspoons baking powder
¾   teaspoon salt
1    egg, lightly beaten
1    cup milk, any variety
2    tablespoons olive oil

Preheat oven to 375. In a large bowl, combine the flour, cornmeal, wheat germ, sugar if desired, baking powder and salt. In a small bowl, whisk together the egg, milk and olive oil. Make a well in the dry ingredients, add liquid mixture and stir just to combine. Fold in desired addition* or top with pepper jam by making an indentation in each muffin. Spoon batter into a greased muffin tin and bake for 12-15 minutes. Brown the tops of muffins on broil for 1-2 minutes.

*¾  cup dried cranberries
*½  cup sun-dried tomatoes
*½  cup flaxseeds
*½  cup thinly slice scallions
*¾  cup chopped peanuts
*5  teaspoons pepper jam

# OVEN BAKED PANCAKE

## Serves 2-4

I find this dish both romantic and intriguing. To make it a complete meal, serve with fresh fruit and cottage cheese or select a protein rich breakfast meat.

2　　eggs
½　　cup white flour
½　　cup milk, any variety
¼　　teaspoon salt
½　　teaspoon vanilla
¼　　teaspoon cinnamon
1　　tablespoon canola oil
Butter and syrup if desired as a topping

Preheat oven to 475. In a medium bowl with electric beaters, beat the eggs until pale yellow. Whisk in flour, whisk until fully incorporated, add milk, salt, vanilla and cinnamon. Pour canola oil into a pie plate and heat in oven for 5 minutes. Remove pie plate from oven, pour batter into plate, and bake in the middle of the oven for 15 minutes or until golden brown and puffed.

# HEARTY WHOLE WHEAT BREAD

# 1 Loaf

The toasted millet and the flaxseeds, makes for a nourishing loaf and a tasty bread.

| | |
|---|---|
| 1 | package active dry yeast |
| 1 | teaspoon sugar |
| 1¾ | cups warm water, divided use |
| 2 | tablespoons molasses |
| 2 | teaspoons salt |
| 2 | tablespoons olive oil |
| ½ | cup toasted millet |
| ½ | cup flaxseeds |
| 4-4½ | cups whole-wheat flour |

In a large bowl, dissolve yeast and sugar; add ½ cup warm water. Allow mixture to proof for about 5 minutes. Add remaining 1¼ cups of water, molasses, salt, oil, millet and flaxseeds, stir well. Add 2 cups of flour and mix well. Continue to stir adding a little flour at a time until you have a dough that becomes stiff and pulls away from the sides of the bowl. Turn onto a floured surface and knead about 5-7 minutes or until dough becomes smooth and elastic. Shape the dough into a loaf and place in an oiled 9x5 inch bread pan. Cover bread with a kitchen towel and allow to rise in a warm draft free spot until doubled in bulk, about 1 hour. Bake in a preheated 350 oven for 45-50 minutes or until loaf sounds hollow when tapped on the bottom.

# OLIVE BREAD

## 2 medium loaves

Although the ingredients are similar to the olive muffins, the two do not compare. Slices of this bread are good with cream cheese and roasted vegetables or make a sandwich of it with fresh turkey or chicken. This loaf is also delicious toasted and served alongside scrambled eggs.

2     packages active dry yeast
½     teaspoon sugar
2     cups warm water, divided use
3     tablespoons olive oil
2     teaspoons salt
1½   cups whole-wheat flour
2     cups Kalamata olives, pitted and chopped
3-4  cups white flour

In a large bowl, combine yeast and sugar with a ⅓ cup warm water and proof the mixture until foamy. Stir in the remaining 1⅔ cups water, olive oil and salt. Add the whole-wheat flour and stir to combine, fold in olives. Add white flour one cup at a time, mixing well after each addition. Knead the dough adding more flour to keep it from sticking, knead until the dough is smooth and elastic about 8-10 minutes. Place dough in a large bowl coated with oil, turn dough to oil the surface. Cover and let it rise in a warm draft free spot until doubled in bulk, about 1½ hours. Punch dough down and divide into 2 loaves, shape the loaves and place in 2 oiled 9x5x3-inch tins and allow to rise for about 45 minutes or until doubled in bulk. Bake the bread in a 350 oven for 40-45 minutes or until it sounds hollow when the bottom is tapped.

# Miscellany

The enhancers! Several of the recipes in this chapter are just that, they enhance the flavor of something bland or act as a spread or sauce for tossed green salads, chicken, seafood, meat, pasta and cheese. All the recipes in this chapter can be prepared in advance.

Better Butter
Flaky Pie Crust
Won Ton Chips
Celery Seed Dressing
Maple Cranberry Sauce
Honey-Curry Glazed Pineapple
Garlic Oatmeal "Croutons"
Peach Marmalade
Sesame Ginger Dressing
Apple Barbecue Sauce
Sweet and Sour Salad Dressing
Creamy Salad Dressing
Pesto

# BETTER BUTTER

## 1 cup

The best of both worlds, you nearly get the entire butter flavor, but with just half the fat. Allow the butter to soften before you blend it. You can easily make two batches.

1    stick, ½ cup butter
½    cup olive or canola oil or a mixture of both
2    tablespoons water, optional

In a medium bowl with a wire whisk or in a food processor, blend butter, oil, and water until well combined. Refrigerate better butter before using.

# FLAKY PIE CRUST

## One single pie crust

I store my flour in the freezer and I believe the secret to this flaky crust is the cold flour. Surprisingly, oil replaces the usual shortening that is often found in pie crust recipes.

1    cup white flour, *cold*
⅛    cup raw wheat germ
½    teaspoon salt
¼    cup canola or soy oil, *cold*
2½   tablespoons *cold water**

In a large bowl, combine white flour, wheat germ and salt. Pour oil over flour and "toss" until flour mixture is course. Slowly drizzle in cold water. Knead dough a *few* times to fully incorporate ingredients. Refrigerate for 30 minutes.

Preheat oven to 425. Roll dough between two sheets of wax paper. Carefully place dough into a 9-inch pie plate and make a fluted edge with the dough that laps over edges. Prick the shell with a fork in several places to ensure even baking and bake for 12-15 minutes or until light brown.

*    damp weather and humidity seem to affect dough coming together, add more water (a little at a time) if dough seems dry

# WON TON CHIPS

## Yields 200 triangles*

The crispness of these chips is similar to the crispness of a potato chip, but the flavor is all together different. Vege-Sal is a vegetable/salt seasoning available from a health food store. These chips are suitable for just about anything that calls for crackers and they are a good choice if you are serving a dip. If stored in an airtight container, won ton chips will last for several days.

1 package won ton wrappers
Olive oil
Salt or Vege-Sal

Preheat oven to 400. Arrange won tons in a single layer not touching one another on a cookie sheet. Brush with olive oil and lightly season with salt, Vege-Sal or desired herbs. Carefully cut each square from one corner to the other making four triangles. Bake for 6-8 minutes or until lightly brown WATCH CLOSELY as they brown very quickly. Cool on baking sheet for 1-2 minutes.

\*    prepare any desired amount of won tons, one package yields about 200 crackers.

# CELERY SEED DRESSING

## Yields 1½ cups

This dressing is delicious tossed with salad greens, cold pasta dishes and fruit. It will last for several days in the refrigerator.

⅓    cup sugar
1     teaspoon salt
1     teaspoon dry mustard
1     teaspoon fresh minced onion
¼    cup apple cider vinegar
1     cup canola oil
1     teaspoon celery seed

In a medium bowl, combine sugar, salt and dry mustard. Add onion and vinegar. Gradually add oil in a slow stream, whisk constantly until mixture is fully emulsified. Stir in celery seeds. Serve dressing at room temperature.

# MAPLE CRANBERRY SAUCE

## About 2½-3 cups

I not only serve this as a side dish with turkey dinner but it is delicious as a spread for chicken or turkey sandwiches and beautiful spooned over vanilla frozen yogurt. It is a snap to put together. Prepare it in advance if necessary, it will last for several days in the refrigerator.

One 12-ounce bag fresh cranberries, rinsed
1    cup pure maple syrup
1    cup cranberry-raspberry juice
Grated zest of one orange
1    cup walnuts, chopped

In a medium saucepan, combine cranberries, maple syrup, juice and orange zest. Bring mixture to a boil, lower heat and cook until cranberries pop open, about 10 minutes. Allow to cool before adding walnuts.

# HONEY-CURRY GLAZED PINEAPPLE

## Serves 4-6

Serve as an accompaniment to sliced baked ham or spoon over frozen vanilla yogurt or ice cream.

1   pineapple, peeled, cored and cut into bite size pieces
¼   cup honey
1   tablespoon curry powder
1   tablespoon vanilla extract
¼   cup light brown sugar, packed
¼   cup Grand Marnier liqueur

Preheat oven to 500. In a medium bowl, combine pineapple, honey, curry powder and vanilla, toss to coat ingredients well. Arrange on a baking sheet and bake for 10 minutes. Remove and sprinkle pineapple evenly with brown sugar and Grand Marnier. Light a long match, ignite mixture and serve immediately.

# GARLIC OATMEAL "CROUTONS"

I got the idea for these "croutons" when my husband and I were cutting back on carbohydrates. The savory sweet combination works with almost any salad combination.

¼   cup olive oil
¼   cup honey
¼   cup garlic, minced (about 5 large cloves)
½   cup rolled oats

Preheat oven to 350. In a small bowl, combine olive oil, honey, garlic and oatmeal; stir until well combined. Spread on a cookie sheet and bake for 10 minutes. With a metal spatula, turn "croutons" and bake an additional 5-10 minutes or until chestnut brown. Turn again before allowing to cool on baking sheet. Once cool, break apart "croutons" with metal spatula. Store in an airtight container. "Croutons" will keep for several days.

# PEACH MARMALADE

## Yields about five 8-ounce jars

I prepare this recipe when summer peaches are plentiful.

2    oranges, unpeeled and quartered
½    lemon, unpeeled
6    medium peaches, peeled and chopped
3½ cups sugar

Place oranges and lemon in food processor, and pulse until mixture is chopped. In a large container combine peaches and orange/lemon mixture, add sugar and mix well. Refrigerate and let stand overnight. Place marmalade in a large saucepan and allow to come to room temperature, bring to a boil and boil for 20 minutes, stirring frequently. Pour into sterilized jars and seal.

# SESAME GINGER DRESSING

## 1 cup

A delicious compliment when tossed with a combination of cold Soba noodles, assorted chopped vegetables and cooked chicken or shrimp. It makes a great dipping sauce for the Green Onion Won Ton Rounds found on page 136, or as a sauce to accompany egg rolls. It will keep for more than a week stored in the refrigerator.

¼    cup fresh gingerroot, peeled
⅓    cup canola oil
3    tablespoons honey
3    tablespoons tamari or soy sauce
2    tablespoons seasoned rice vinegar
1    tablespoon *dark* sesame oil
Salt and pepper to taste
2    tablespoons sesame seeds, toasted

In a blender or food processor, combine gingerroot, oil, honey, tamari or soy sauce, vinegar, and sesame oil. Blend until smooth, season with salt and pepper. Stir in sesame seeds.

# APPLE BARBECUE SAUCE

## Yields 1⅓ cups

A zesty flavor-booster for steak, fish, chicken, shrimp and spare ribs.

½  cup apple jelly
One 8-ounce can tomato sauce
¼  cup apple cider vinegar
2  tablespoons brown sugar
2  tablespoons water
1  teaspoon Tabasco or hot sauce
¼  teaspoon salt

In a medium saucepan, combine jelly, tomato sauce, vinegar, sugar, water, Tabasco and salt. Bring mixture to a boil and stir until smooth. Reduce heat and simmer, stirring occasionally for about a ½ hour.

# SWEET AND SOUR SALAD DRESSING

# Yields 1 cup

This dressing is especially good poured over wedges of iceberg lettuce. For optimum flavor prepare a day in advance.

½    cup canola oil
⅓    cup sugar
4    tablespoons apple cider vinegar
2    tablespoons ketchup
2    tablespoons grated onion
½    teaspoon celery seed
½    teaspoon dry mustard
1    teaspoon salt
¼    teaspoon paprika

Place ingredients in a food processor and process until smooth. Chill overnight before serving.

# CREAMY SALAD DRESSING

## ⅔ cup

This simple to prepare dressing is abundant with flavor and compliments the ordinary and often bland cold pasta salad. It is also a delicious spread for steak, chicken or vegetable sandwiches. This recipe doubles well and is a good keeper.

½  cup mayonnaise
1  tablespoon rice vinegar
1  tablespoon soy sauce
1  tablespoon Dijon mustard
1  tablespoon dark sesame oil

In a small bowl, combine mayonnaise, vinegar, soy sauce, mustard and sesame oil. Whisk ingredients until smooth.

# PESTO

## About 1 cup

I particularly like pesto served with the Zucchini Pancakes recipe on page 135 and it is a necessary component in the Pesto Cheese Torte found in the Appetizer's with Cheese section. You may also toss this with the Basil-Shrimp Pasta dish on page 84; simply omit the dressing called for in the recipe.

2½   cups firmly packed fresh basil leaves
2     large garlic cloves
½    cup chopped almonds
½    cup fresh grated Parmesan cheese
½    cup olive oil
Salt to taste

In a food processor, combine basil leaves, garlic cloves, chopped almonds and Parmesan cheese. Drizzle olive oil through feed tube and whirl mixture until well combined. Season with salt.

# Chocolate Desserts

If you love chocolate this chapter offers twelve moist, crunchy, melt in your mouth chocolate desserts. Some make excellent hostess gifts, while others like the Chocolate Beet Cake will fool your guests! Many recipes in this chapter are a reflection of my philosophy that is throughout the cookbook, successfully replacing oil for butter, skim milk for cream and cocoa for chocolate.

Chocolate Beet Cake
Yum, Yum Dessert
Stove to Oven Brownies
Chocolate Bread Pudding
Buttermilk Cake
Chocolate Chip Peanut Butter Bars
Chocolate Truffles
Creamy Chocolate Baby Cakes
Cocoa Pudding in a Cake
Mysterious Butter Crunch
Chocolate Covered Rice Crispies
Chocolate Meringue Pie
Chocolate Oatmeal Crunch

# CHOCOLATE BEET CAKE

## Serves 6-8

I have prepared this moist cake countless times and no one has ever guessed that beets are one of the main ingredients! Buy small beets they usually do not have the woodsy flavor sometimes found in root vegetables.

## CAKE

1    cup white flour
⅔    cup sugar
¼    cup unsweetened cocoa powder
1    teaspoon baking soda
⅛    teaspoon salt
¼    cup low fat sour cream
3    tablespoons canola oil
1    egg, lightly beaten
½    teaspoon vanilla
¼    cup reserved beet water
2    medium beets (1 cup) cooked until tender, peeled and shredded

## ICING

One 4-ounce package low fat cream cheese, at room temperature
½    cup confectioners' sugar
¼    teaspoon vanilla

Preheat oven to 350. In a large mixing bowl, combine, flour, sugar, cocoa powder, baking soda and salt. In a medium bowl, whisk until well combined, sour cream, oil, egg, vanilla and reserved beet water. Add sour cream mixture to flour mixture and stir until well combined. Fold in shredded beets. Spoon batter into a lightly oiled 8-inch round cake pan and bake for 22 minutes or until toothpick inserted in center of cake comes out clean. Allow cake to cool before transferring to a platter. In a small bowl, whisk together cream cheese, confectioners' sugar and vanilla. Spread icing evenly over cake.

# YUM, YUM DESSERT

## 32 squares (about 2x3 inches)

This dessert is perfect for a large crowd and covers the gamut for those with a fondness for sweets—gooey, chocolaty, nutty, cake like and gratifying. You can prepare it the day *before* you plan to serve it.

½   cup butter, softened
¼   cup canola oil
1½ cups sugar
3   eggs
1   teaspoon vanilla
1⅓ cups white flour
½   teaspoon baking powder
½   teaspoon salt
3   tablespoons cocoa powder
One 10.5-ounce bag miniature marshmallows
One 12-ounce bag semi-sweet chocolate chips
1   cup natural chunky peanut butter
2   cups crisp rice cereal

Preheat oven to 350. In a large bowl, cream butter with oil, add sugar. Beat in eggs one at a time, add vanilla and beat until fluffy. In a medium bowl, combine flour, baking powder, salt and cocoa. Add flour mixture to wet ingredients and combine well. Spread in an 11½ x 16½ x 1-inch greased jellyroll pan and bake for 15 minutes. Remove and sprinkle marshmallows evenly over cake, return cake to oven for 2 minutes. Working quickly spread melted marshmallows over cake. (The marshmallows will not spread perfectly). In a medium saucepan, over low heat melt chocolate chips and peanut butter. Stir mixture to combine well. Remove from heat and stir in rice cereal. Spread mixture over cake. Allow cake to cool, chill before cutting.

# STOVE TO OVEN BROWNIES

## Sixteen 2x2-inch squares

These brownies can be prepared in the same amount of time it takes for the oven to preheat. Some say a brownie is a brownie, I always thought this as well, until I tasted this brownie.

½   cup (1 stick) butter
2    squares unsweetened baking chocolate (2-ounces)
1    cup sugar
2    eggs, lightly beaten
½   cup white flour
1    teaspoon vanilla

Preheat oven to 350. In a medium saucepan over medium low heat, melt butter and chocolate. Remove from heat and add sugar, eggs, flour and vanilla *stirring after the addition of each item*. Oil an 8x8x2-inch baking pan and dust with cocoa powder. Pour brownie batter into pan and bake for 22 minutes or until toothpick inserted in center comes out clean.

# CHOCOLATE BREAD PUDDING

## Serves 8

This bread pudding is divine!

5    cups French or Italian bread cut or pulled apart into bite size
     pieces
One 6-ounce package semi-sweet chocolate chips
3    cups warm milk, any variety
1    egg, lightly beaten
⅓    cup sugar
1    teaspoon vanilla
1    teaspoon cinnamon
¼    teaspoon salt

Preheat oven to 350. In a 2-quart baking dish, combine bread,
chocolate chips and milk. Soak mixture for 15 minutes. In a medium
bowl, combine egg, sugar, vanilla, cinnamon and salt, add to soaked
bread mixture. Stir gently with a fork until well blended. (Baking
will distribute the chips evenly). Set baking dish in a larger pan of
hot water and bake uncovered for 45 minutes. Serve warm with
vanilla frozen yogurt or ice cream.

# BUTTERMILK CAKE

## Yields 12 servings

For this recipe, I use canola oil instead of butter and am amazed that I cannot tell the difference. Whatever your choice, both make a moist and delicious cake. This cake is simple to prepare, and can be mixed in one bowl. If you do not have buttermilk, add 1 teaspoon lemon juice or white vinegar to a ½ cup of milk.

1    cup of canola oil *or* 1 stick butter
1    cup of water
½    cup of low fat buttermilk
4    tablespoons of cocoa
2    cups of sugar
2    cups of white flour
2    eggs, well beaten
1    teaspoon of baking soda
1    teaspoon vanilla
½    cup confectioners' sugar mixed with 1-2 teaspoons of water

Preheat oven to 350. In a medium saucepan, combine butter *or* canola oil, water, buttermilk, cocoa and sugar. Bring mixture to a boil, remove from heat and whisk in flour a ½ cup at a time, combine well after each addition. Whisk in eggs, baking soda and vanilla. Pour into a greased 9x12 inch-baking pan. Bake in a 350 oven for 30 minutes. In a small bowl, combine the confectioners' sugar with the water adding more or less water depending on the desired consistency. Allow cake to cool before drizzling icing over cake.

# CHOCOLATE CHIP

# PEANUT BUTTER BARS

## 16 squares

These bars are so tasty I usually double the recipe. Like most desserts of this kind, these bars freeze well.

¼   cup butter, softened
¼   cup chunky peanut butter
½   cup sugar
1   egg
1   teaspoon vanilla
½   cup flour
½   teaspoon baking powder
¼   teaspoon salt
One 6-ounce package chocolate chips

Preheat oven to 350. In a large bowl, beat together butter, peanut butter and sugar. Add egg and vanilla, beat until smooth. Stir in flour, baking powder and salt; combine well. Fold in chocolate chips. Spoon ingredients into an 8x2x2-inch greased baking pan. Bake for 25 minutes. Cool before cutting into squares.

# CHOCOLATE TRUFFLES

## About 20 one-inch balls

These truffles make a lovely hostess gift and are especially pretty if put in decorative Bon Bon size paper party cups. It is best to prepare the truffle mixture a day in advance. Choose your favorite liqueur; favorites are Grand Marnier, Kahlua or Cointreau.

6-ounces sweet German chocolate
4    tablespoons butter
2    tablespoons milk, any variety
2    tablespoons liqueur
Cocoa powder
Confectioners' sugar, optional

In a medium saucepan, over moderately low heat, melt chocolate, butter, milk and liqueur. Stir mixture until well combined. Refrigerate overnight. Roll into a ball about one heaping teaspoon of truffle mixture between the palms of your hands. Roll each ball into cocoa powder. If desired, lightly dust truffles with confectioners' sugar.

# CREAMY CHOCOLATE BABY CAKES

## About 90 mini cakes

A moist cake with a creamy center. I use the 2-inch mini paper muffin cups. These mini cakes freeze beautifully.

### CREAM CENTER

1   egg
One 4-ounce package light cream cheese
⅓   cup sugar
⅛   teaspoon salt
One 6-ounce bag chocolate chips

### CHOCOLATE CAKE

1½   cups white flour
1   cup sugar
¼   cup cocoa
1   teaspoon baking soda
½   teaspoon salt
1   cup water
½   cup oil
2   tablespoons fresh lemon juice
1   teaspoon vanilla

Preheat oven to 350. In a medium bowl, beat until smooth the egg, cream cheese, sugar and salt. Fold in the chocolate chips. In a large bowl sift together the flour, sugar, cocoa, baking soda and salt. In a medium bowl, whisk the water, oil, lemon juice and vanilla together, add to the cocoa mixture and mix until well combined. With a small spoon, fill mini muffin cup ½ full with chocolate mixture. Drop about a ½ teaspoon or more of the creamy center filling into the center of the chocolate mixture. Carefully place mini cups on a baking sheet (muffin cups should not touch one another) and bake for 15-20 minutes.

# COCOA PUDDING IN A CAKE

## Serves 4-6

This cake is best hot, right from the oven. It is also best to prepare just before baking, you can however, combine the dry ingredients in advance. Serve with frozen vanilla yogurt or ice cream.

1    cup white flour
⅔    cup sugar
¼    cup cocoa powder
2    teaspoons baking powder
¼    teaspoon salt
½    cup milk, any variety
3    tablespoons canola oil
1    teaspoon vanilla
1½  cups boiling water

Preheat oven to 350. In a large bowl, combine flour, sugar, cocoa powder, baking powder and salt. In a small bowl, whisk together milk, oil and vanilla, add to dry ingredients. Spoon the batter into a greased 8-inch square-baking pan. Boil 1½ cups of water and pour over cake, DO NOT STIR and bake for 30 minutes or until cake springs back when lightly touched.

# MYSTERIOUS BUTTER CRUNCH

# 38 pieces

This is simple and delicious.

38  unsalted Uneeda Brand Biscuits
2   sticks butter
1   cup light brown sugar, packed
6-ounce package semi-sweet chocolate chips

Preheat oven to 350. Line a 15x30-inch cookie sheet with the biscuits. In a medium saucepan, over moderate heat, melt butter, add brown sugar, reduce heat and allow mixture to come to a boil stirring constantly. Pour mixture over crackers and bake for 5-6 minutes. Remove from oven and sprinkle with chocolate chips, let stand for a few minutes before spreading chocolate evenly across top of biscuits. Cool completely and break into ragged pieces.

# CHOCOLATE COVERED RICE CRISPIES

## About 70 balls

These make a great hostess gift.

½   cup butter, 1 stick
3   cups rice crispies
1   box confectioners' sugar
One 18-ounce jar chunky peanut butter
One 12-ounce bag chocolate chips
¼   bar of paraffin wax

In a large saucepan melt the butter over moderate heat; add rice crispies, confectioners' sugar and peanut butter. Combine and distribute ingredients evenly. In a double boiler melt chocolate chips and paraffin wax over low heat. Shape rice crispy mixture into about 70 balls and dip them into melted chocolate, place on a wax paper lined cookie sheet. Allow to cool in the refrigerator before placing in an airtight container.

# CHOCOLATE MERINGUE PIE

# Serves 6

A delicious pie that melts in your mouth.

## CRUST

2   egg whites (room temperature)
½   cup sugar
⅛   teaspoon cream of tartar
½   cup chopped nuts, pecans, walnuts or almonds

## FILLING

¾   cup semi-sweet chocolate chips
3   tablespoons hot water
½   teaspoon vanilla
1   cup whipping cream

Preheat oven to 275. Lightly oil a 9-inch pie dish. In a medium bowl, with an electric beater, beat egg whites on high speed and gradually add sugar. Add cream of tartar and beat until egg whites are glossy and stiff peaks have formed. Spoon meringue into pie dish, spread evenly across the bottom and sides of dish making a "crust." Sprinkle nuts over top of meringue and bake for 1 hour. In a saucepan, over moderate heat combine chocolate chips and hot water, stir until chocolate has melted and mixture is smooth. Cool mixture, stir in vanilla. Place a medium bowl and beaters in the freezer for about 5 minutes or the refrigerator for about 2 hours. Remove bowl and beater and add whipping cream, beat on high speed until thick. Cream should fall in soft globs or have soft peaks, if you over whip the cream it will turn to butter. Fold whipped cream into chocolate mixture and combine until well blended. Spoon mixture into cooled meringue and spread evenly, chill pie for 2-3 hours before serving.

# CHOCOLATE OATMEAL CRUNCH

## 24 squares

I use almonds in this recipe, but these bars are delicious without nuts.

½   cup butter (1 stick)
½   cup light corn syrup
½   teaspoon salt
2    teaspoons vanilla
¾   cup brown sugar
3    cups quick cooking oats
One 12-ounce package semi-sweet chocolate chips
½   cup chopped nuts, optional

Preheat oven to 350. In a medium saucepan, melt butter over moderate heat; remove from heat and add syrup, salt, vanilla, brown sugar and oats, mix thoroughly. Press mixture into a 13x9-inch baking pan. Bake for 18 minutes. Remove and sprinkle evenly with chocolate chips. Bake for an additional 2 minutes. With a knife, spread chocolate evenly over top of oatmeal mixture. Sprinkle with nuts if desired. Cool before cutting into squares.

# Cakes, Pies, Cookies, Cookie Bars, and Surprises

In this chapter many of the cake and pie recipes main ingredient is from a fruit or vegetable. As I point out in Tips, Alternatives and Suggestions, I seldom purchase fruits and/or vegetables out of their season. Buying them out of season taxes the environment and furthermore the flavor is not at its peak, which will have an effect on the outcome of the recipe. Most cakes and pies are best prepared the day you plan to serve them, the cookies and cookie bars, however, can effectively be prepared in advance and frozen until ready to use.

Mango Cake with Cardamom
Ginger Molasses Cookies
Strawberry Pie
Pecan Squares
Mystery Cake
Tipsy Flummeries
Lemon or Lime Pie
Marinated Fruit with Ginger Stuffed Dates
Spaghetti Squash Cake
Molasses Pie
Sugar Cookies
Lemon Coconut Bars
Peach and Almond Delight
Parsnip Cake
Stay Up All Night Cookies
Peaches and Cream Supreme
Fresh Peach Crisp
Cherry Cobbler
Blueberry Almond Coffeecake
Pear Cake
Autumn Apple Crisp

# MANGO CAKE WITH CARDAMOM

## Serves 8

The idea for this recipe came to me when I had too many ripe mangoes in my fruit basket. The combination of mango with the aromatic cardamom made for a delicious taste-treat dessert. A ripe mango is orange-yellow and rosy blush in color, it will give slightly when light pressure is applied. Mangoes take about 3-4 days to fully ripen.

1    cup peeled mango* cut into bite size pieces (about 2 medium mangoes)
½    cup raspberry cranberry juice
2    eggs
⅔    cup sugar
1    teaspoon vanilla
¼    cup butter, melted
¼    cup canola oil
1    cup flour
½    teaspoon ground cardamom
Confectioners' sugar, optional

Preheat oven to 400. Lightly cover a 10-inch baking dish with cooking spray. Distribute mango evenly in the bottom of baking dish and pour raspberry cranberry juice over fruit. In a large bowl, beat eggs and gradually add the sugar; mix until well combined. Add vanilla, butter and oil, beat until well combined. Stir in flour and cardamom. Spoon batter over fruit mixture, (fruit will show through in some places, cooking will distribute the batter evenly). Bake cake for 20 minutes or until light brown and bubbly. Allow cake to cool, sprinkle with confectioners' sugar if desired.

\*    To get to the flesh of the mango, cut lengthwise as close to the pit as possible, score cut sides of each piece in a crosshatch pattern, turn it inside out, then cut the mango from the skin.

# GINGER MOLASSES COOKIES

## 30 cookies

I am partial to anything that calls for ginger. Ginger in any form, fresh, powdered or crystallized is great for your digestive system.

5 tablespoons butter, softened
⅔ cup light brown sugar, packed
¼ cup molasses
1 egg
2 tablespoons crystallized ginger, chopped well
1⅓ cups white flour
¾ cup toasted wheat germ (watch the wheat germ when toasting it burns quickly)
2 teaspoons baking soda
1½ teaspoons powdered ginger
1 teaspoon cinnamon
2 tablespoons sugar

Preheat oven to 350. In a large bowl cream butter and add brown sugar ⅓ cup at a time. Add molasses and egg, beat until light and fluffy. Stir in crystallized ginger. In a medium bowl, combine flour, wheat germ, baking soda, powdered ginger and cinnamon. Add to molasses mixture and combine well. Cover dough and freeze for 20 minutes or refrigerate for 1 hour. Lightly oil hands and shape the dough into 30 balls about 1 tablespoon each. Roll the balls into the sugar and place on a greased baking sheet and bake for 10-12 minutes*. Allow to cool for 1-2 minutes on baking sheet before removing to wire rack.

* Cookies will appear as though they are not fully baked, baking them longer will result in a tough cookie

172        KERRY DUNNINGTON

# STRAWBERRY PIE

# 6 servings

This pie is rich of color and flavor. I only prepare this recipe when strawberries are in the peak of their season.

One 9-inch baked pie shell (recipe on page 143)
2     tablespoons melted butter
¼    cup plus one tablespoon sugar
4    cups fresh, sliced strawberries, divided use
1    cup water, divided use
2    tablespoons cornstarch
Lemon yogurt, whipped cream or vanilla ice cream to accompany if
    desired

While the pie crust is still warm, pour melted butter over shell and sprinkle with 1 tablespoon sugar, set aside and allow to cool before filling. Fill pie shell evenly with 2 cups of the strawberries. In a medium saucepan, bring ½ cup of water to a boil; add remaining 2 cups of strawberries and ¼ cup sugar; cook over medium heat for 3-5 minutes. In a small bowl, mix ½ cup *cold* water with the cornstarch, stir into hot strawberry mixture, stir until thick. Pour over strawberries. Chill until ready to serve.

# PECAN SQUARES

## Twenty-four 2x2-inch squares

These are decadent! If pecans are too rich, you can successfully prepare these with equal amounts of chopped pecans, walnuts and almonds. For a unique dessert-bar-bite, cut each square on the diagonal for a triangular shape.

## CRUST

2    sticks butter, 1 cup, softened
⅔    cup sugar
2    cups white flour

## TOPPING

11    tablespoons butter
⅛    cup maple syrup
⅛    cup honey
¼    cup molasses
3    tablespoons milk, any variety
½    cup brown sugar
3½    cups pecans, chopped

Preheat oven to 350. In a food processor combine the butter, sugar and flour—pulse the mixture until the dough is the consistency of cookie dough. Press evenly into a greased 9x12-inch baking pan and bake for 20 minutes. In a medium saucepan, over moderate heat, combine butter, maple syrup, honey, molasses, milk, and brown sugar. Stir mixture until melted and well combined. Pour evenly over crust. Distribute pecans evenly over syrup mixture and gently press pecans lightly into filling and bake an additional 25 minutes.

# MYSTERY CAKE

## One 9-inch tube cake

The "mystery" my tasters concluded was whatever it was that made this cake so incredibly moist!

3     eggs, separated
1⅔   cups sugar, divided use
1     cup white flour
½     teaspoon salt
½     cup butter (1 stick) melted
1     teaspoon vanilla
½     cup milk, any variety
1½   cups water
2     tablespoons rum, brandy or fruit juice

Preheat oven to 375. In a large bowl, beat egg yolks until light, continue beating and gradually add ⅔ cup of the sugar. Stir in flour, salt, butter, vanilla and milk; mix well. In a medium bowl, beat egg whites until stiff. Fold egg whites into cake batter. Pour into a greased 9-inch tube pan and bake for 30 minutes. While cake is baking, combine water and 1 cup of sugar in a medium saucepan, bring mixture to a slow boil. Cook syrup until thick, stirring frequently, for about 40 minutes (the color will darken slightly as it thickens). Remove from heat, stir in rum, brandy or fruit juice. Allow cake to cool for 10 minutes. Using a chopstick or fork prick several holes in the top of cake and spoon syrup over cake.

# "TIPSY" FLUMMERIES

## Serves 8

These flummeries can be prepared several days in advance, are simple to put together and the presentation is impressive, if you are planning a dinner party this recipe is a good choice. I named them "tipsy" flummeries because the flavor of the Cointreau is rather pronounced. If you want to offer a spot of chocolate, accompany the flummery with a chocolate truffle, recipe on page 162.

One envelope unflavored gelatin
½    cup Cointreau, plus two tablespoons to marinate orange peel
2    cups heavy cream
⅓    cup sugar, plus 1 tablespoon
Fresh seasonal fruit for garnish (kiwi, raspberries, pineapple and
     orange sections are a colorful combination)
Orange peel from one orange

Lightly grease eight ½ cup molds. In a small bowl, sprinkle gelatin over ½ cup Cointreau. In a medium pan, over moderate heat, heat cream and ⅓ cup sugar, stir mixture and heat until sugar has dissolved. Remove from heat and stir in thickened gelatin mixture. Stir until well combined. Fill each mold about three quarters full. Allow flummeries to cool before covering and chilling. With a fruit peeler, peel rind from orange. In a small bowl, cover orange peel with 2 tablespoons Cointreau, marinate for several hours. Dip peel in sugar, set aside until ready to garnish.

To remove flummeries from mold, dip into warm water for 1-2 minutes, invert onto dessert plate and jiggle mold until the flummery comes away from the sides of the mold, garnish with fruit and orange peel.

# LEMON OR LIME PIE

## 6 servings

Whether you choose lemon or lime, this makes a refreshing dessert. If you prepare this in the morning, refrigerate the pie until serving time.

1    baked piecrust (recipe on page 143 or a frozen pie crust baked according to package directions)
One 15-ounce can sweetened condensed milk, regular or low fat
1    tablespoon coarsely grated lemon or lime peel
½    cup *fresh* lemon or lime juice
¼    teaspoon salt
2    eggs, separated
2    tablespoons sugar

Preheat oven to 350. In a medium bowl, combine sweetened condensed milk, peel, juice, salt, and egg yolks, stir until ingredients are fully incorporated. Pour into baked pie shell. In a large bowl, beat egg whites, gradually add sugar and beat until stiff. Spoon meringue evenly over pie and with the back of a scraper "lift" the meringue mixture creating small peaks. Bake pie for 10-15 minutes or until meringue is light brown.

# MARINATED FRUIT
# WITH GINGER STUFFED DATES
## Serves 8

I am appreciative when a hostess serves a light dessert after dinner. This recipe fits into that category. Choose seasonal fruit and fruit that varies in color. Fresh dates are available in the produce section of most grocery stores.

Assorted fresh fruit cut into bite size pieces (allow about ¾-1 cup
    per person)
About 8 dates, pitted
About 8 pieces crystallized ginger
2    tablespoons Cointreau, optional

In a medium bowl, combine fruit. Stuff each date with a piece of ginger. Slice each date into thirds, toss with fruit and stir in Cointreau. Refrigerate and allow fruit to marinate for several hours.

# SPAGHETTI SQUASH CAKE

## Serves 6-8

Another vegetable cake in disguise. The refreshing ginger cream icing compliments this moist cake.

¼   cup canola oil
1   egg, lightly beaten
2   tablespoons milk, any variety
½   teaspoon vanilla
1   cup cooked spaghetti squash, finely chopped
1   cup white flour
⅓   cup sugar
⅓   cup packed brown sugar
⅛   teaspoon salt
½   teaspoon cinnamon
½   teaspoon powdered ginger
1   teaspoon baking powder
¼   cup ginger preserves
4   ounces (½ cup) light cream cheese

Preheat oven to 350. In a medium bowl, whisk until well blended canola oil, egg, milk and vanilla. Stir in spaghetti squash. In a large bowl combine flour, sugar, brown sugar, salt, cinnamon, ginger and baking powder. Add squash mixture to flour mixture and combine until moistened and well blended. Spread cake batter into a greased 8-inch round cake pan and bake for 20 minutes or until a toothpick inserted in the center comes out clean. Allow to cool before transferring to a platter. In a small bowl combine ginger preserves with cream cheese, spread evenly over cake.

# MOLASSES PIE

## Serves 6-8

I recommend using a good quality molasses in this recipe.

One 9-inch *unbaked* pie shell, recipe on page 143
1    cup white flour
½    cup, firmly packed brown sugar
¼    cup butter, cut into chunks
1    cup water
1    teaspoon baking soda
1    cup dark molasses
¼    teaspoon salt
Vanilla frozen yogurt or ice cream to accompany if desired

Preheat oven to 375. In a medium bowl combine flour, brown sugar and butter. With the tips of your fingers or with a fork combine mixture until it resembles course meal. In a medium saucepan, bring water to a boil, remove from heat and stir in baking soda, (mixture will bubble) molasses and salt, combine well. Pour into unbaked pie shell and sprinkle flour mixture evenly over molasses mixture. Bake for 10 minutes; reduce oven temperature to 350 and bake an additional 25-30 minutes. Cool to room temperature before serving.

# SUGAR COOKIES

## About 6 dozen *very thin* cookies*

A more appropriate name would be labor of love cookies. These paper-thin delectable cookies are great around the holidays. Turn on some music and dream about sugarplums while you roll and bake.

2    sticks butter (1 cup) softened
1    cup sugar
1    egg, lightly beaten
1    tablespoon milk
½    teaspoon vanilla
1½  cups flour
1    teaspoon baking powder
½    teaspoon salt
Additional flour and sugar for rolling dough
1    egg white lightly beaten
Powdered cinnamon, and or red and green colored sugar to dust the
      tops of cookies

In a large bowl, cream butter and gradually add sugar. Add egg, milk and vanilla. In a medium bowl, combine flour, baking powder and salt, slowly add flour mixture to butter mixture and combine until you have a well-incorporated cookie dough. Refrigerate for 1½ hours or overnight.

Preheat oven to 350. Sprinkle an equal mixture of flour and sugar on the surface you are going to roll the dough. Divide dough into 6 sections; roll a section at a time into a paper-thin cookie or the desired thickness you like. Cut into shapes and place on a greased cookie sheet. With a pastry brush, brush the tops of each cookie with egg white and sprinkle with desired topping and bake for 10-12 minutes or until light brown.

*    Depends on the desired thickness of the cookie

# LEMON COCONUT BARS

## Yields thirty-five 2x2-inch squares

If you like coconut, raisins and walnuts this dessert bar is for you.

## CRUST

2   sticks butter, (1 cup), softened
⅔   cup sugar
2   cups white flour

## TOPPING

3    eggs
1    cup packed brown sugar
½    teaspoon salt
⅓    cup fresh lemon juice
2    teaspoons grated lemon rind
1½   cups shredded coconut
½    cup raisins
½    cup chopped walnuts

Preheat oven to 350. In a medium bowl, cream butter, slowly add sugar, gradually add flour—the mixture should be the consistency of cookie dough. Press dough into a greased 9x12-inch baking pan and bake for 20 minutes. In a large bowl, beat eggs until bright yellow; add brown sugar, salt, lemon juice and lemon rind. Beat mixture until well combined. In a medium bowl, combine coconut, raisins and walnuts. Pour egg/lemon mixture over crust to cover completely. Spread coconut mixture evenly over filling. Press mixture lightly into the filling and bake for an additional 25 minutes. Allow to cool before cutting. For the best cutting results, cover and refrigerate overnight.

# PEACH AND ALMOND DELIGHT

## Serves 6

This dessert has a homemade looking presentation. It is good with a dollop of frozen raspberry yogurt.

1   cup plus 2 tablespoons white flour
¼   cup wheat germ
6   tablespoons sugar, divided use
¼   teaspoon salt
⅓   cup canola oil
2   tablespoons cold water
½   cup ground almonds
4   medium peaches, about 2 pounds, peeled and thinly sliced
2   tablespoons butter, cut into small pieces

In a large bowl, combine 1 cup flour, wheat germ, 1 tablespoon sugar and salt. Drizzle oil over flour mixture and "toss" with a fork allowing flour to grab oil resulting in large chunks. Add water and knead a few times. Gather the dough into a ball, cover and refrigerate for 30 minutes or overnight. Preheat oven to 375. Roll the dough into a 14-inch diameter and transfer to a greased cookie sheet. In a small bowl, combine 2 tablespoons flour, 4 tablespoons sugar and almonds. Sprinkle almond mixture evenly over the dough. Arrange peach slices in the center of the dough leaving about a 1-2-inch border. Fold the edges over the peaches (the center will remain exposed) sprinkle with remaining 1 tablespoon of sugar and dot with butter. Bake for 45 minutes or until peaches are bubbly and crust is golden brown.

# PARSNIP CAKE

## Serves 8

Choose small, firm parsnips, the larger variety have a woodsy flavor. This is a surprisingly moist cake and your tasters will never know the vegetable ingredient. This recipe doubles nicely. To make muffins, lightly oil 8 muffin cups, fill each cup almost to the top, and bake for about 18 minutes.

## CAKE

1   cup white flour
⅔   cup sugar
1   teaspoon baking powder
⅛   teaspoon salt
¼   cup plain low fat yogurt
3   tablespoons vegetable or canola oil
2   teaspoons grated orange rind
½   teaspoon vanilla
1   egg
1   cup parsnips, peeled and shredded (about 2 medium)

## ICING

4-ounces (½ cup) light cream cheese
½   cup confectioners' sugar
¼   teaspoon vanilla
Orange rind strips for garnish

Preheat oven to 350. In a large bowl, combine flour, sugar, baking powder and salt. In a medium bowl, whisk together yogurt, oil, orange rind, vanilla and egg. Make a well in the center of dry ingredients and add liquid ingredients, combine until moistened. Fold in parsnips, distribute mixture evenly. Spread batter into a lightly oiled 8-inch round cake pan and bake for 20 minutes or until cake is light brown and toothpick inserted in the center comes out clean.

Allow cake to cool for 10 minutes in pan before removing to a wire rack. In a small bowl, combine cream cheese, confectioners' sugar and vanilla. Beat until mixture is smooth and creamy. When cake has cooled, spread icing over cake and garnish with orange rind strips.

# STAY UP ALL NIGHT COOKIES

## 2½ dozen cookies

These meringues sleep in the oven for 6 hours or overnight. They are delicious served with fresh assorted fruit. The "filler" can be anything you desire; peppermint candy, cocoa powder, or finely chopped nuts, challenge your imagination.

2    egg whites at room temperature
⅔    cup sugar
½    teaspoon vanilla
One 6-ounce package chocolate chips*

Preheat oven to 375. In a large bowl, beat egg whites and gradually add sugar. Beat until mixture is stiff and soft peaks form. Add vanilla. Fold in chocolate chips or desired filling*. Drop by teaspoons on a foil lined baking sheet. Place in the preheated oven, *turn off oven* and "bake" meringues for 6 hours or overnight.

*½    cup finely chopped peppermint candy
*1    tablespoon cocoa powder
*½    cup finely chopped almonds

# PEACHES AND CREAM SUPREME

## Serves 8

This takes a bit of time to prepare and needs to refrigerate for a least 2 hours before serving.

## CAKE

½   cup butter (1 stick), softened
⅔   cup sugar
1   teaspoon vanilla
2   eggs
1   cup flour
1   teaspoon baking powder
¼   teaspoon salt

## FILLING

½   cup (4-ounces) light cream cheese, softened
⅓   cup sugar
¼   cup light sour cream
1   egg
¾   teaspoon salt

## TOPPING

4   cups fresh peaches, peeled and chopped
1   cup light sour cream
¼   cup light brown sugar, packed

Preheat oven to 350. In a medium bowl, cream butter with sugar, add vanilla and eggs and beat until smooth. In a small bowl, combine flour, baking powder and salt. Add to butter mixture and beat until smooth. Spread cake batter into a lightly oiled 10-inch round baking dish, set aside. In a medium bowl, beat cream cheese, sugar, sour cream, egg and salt until well combined. Spoon filling evenly over cake batter. Bake for 30 minutes or until light brown. While cake is baking assemble the topping by combining the sour cream and brown sugar; fold in peaches. Spoon peach mixture evenly over top of filling and bake an additional 5 minutes, allow to cool before you refrigerate for at least two hours before serving.

# FRESH PEACH CRISP

## 6 servings

My favorite juices to use with this recipe are apple cider and/or papaya but feel free to use anything you have. You can whip this together in no time. Place it in the oven just as you sit down for dinner and it will be ready for dessert. Serve it with vanilla frozen yogurt or ice cream, it is delicious however on its own!

4   cups peeled, sliced peaches
½   cup juice (apple, apple cider, papaya or orange juice)
¾   cup white flour
1   cup brown sugar
1   teaspoon cinnamon
½   cup (1 stick) butter cut into chunks

Preheat oven to 350. Arrange peaches in a 9x9-inch baking pan and top with juice. In a medium bowl, combine flour, brown sugar and cinnamon. Drop butter chunks into flour mixture and cut with 2 knives or with fingertips until the mixture is somewhat crumbly. Sprinkle mixture over top of peaches. Bake for 30 minutes or until bubbly.

# CHERRY COBBLER

## Serves 6

When these gems are in season, this recipe is a tasty way to end a summer supper.

5   cups pitted cherries
1   cup sugar, divided
2   tablespoons cornstarch
½   cup water
3   tablespoons butter
1   tablespoon grated lemon rind
¼   teaspoon almond extract
1   cup white flour
1   teaspoon baking powder
½   teaspoon salt
½   cup milk, any variety
¼   cup butter, softened
1   teaspoon vanilla
1   egg

Preheat oven to 350. In a medium saucepan over moderate heat, combine cherries, ½ cup sugar, cornstarch and water. Stirring constantly, bring mixture to a boil and boil for 1 minute. Remove from heat, stir in 3 tablespoons butter, lemon rind and almond extract. Pour mixture into a lightly oiled 11x7-inch baking dish. In a large bowl, combine ½ cup sugar, flour, baking powder and salt. Add milk, butter and vanilla. With an electric mixer, beat mixture at medium speed for 2 minutes. Add egg and beat for an additional 2 minutes. Spoon batter evenly over cherry mixture. Bake cobbler for 40-45 minutes or until golden brown.

# BLUEBERRY ALMOND COFFEECAKE

## Serves 6

Blueberries make this breakfast, brunch or dessert cake moist and the addition of almonds gives it a nice crunch. Serve hot from the oven or at room temperature.

1    cup white flour
½    cup sugar
¾    teaspoon baking powder
½    teaspoon salt
¼    teaspoon baking soda
1    cup fresh blueberries, divided
⅔    cup milk, any variety
2    tablespoons canola oil
1    teaspoon vanilla
¼    teaspoon almond extract
1    egg
¼    cup sliced almonds
1    tablespoon brown sugar
¼    teaspoon cinnamon

Preheat oven to 350. In a large bowl, combine flour, sugar, baking powder, salt, baking soda and ⅔ cup blueberries, toss well. In a small bowl, whisk until well combined milk, oil, vanilla, almond extract, and egg. Add to flour mixture, stir until combined. Spoon batter into an 8-inch square baking pan coated with cooking spray. Top with remaining ⅓ cup blueberries. In a small bowl, combine almonds, brown sugar and cinnamon, sprinkle over blueberries. Bake for 35 minutes or until a toothpick inserted in the center comes out clean.

# PEAR CAKE

## Serves 8

If ripe pears are not available, fresh pineapple cut into bite size pieces makes for a delicious replacement.

2 eggs
⅔ cup sugar
1 teaspoon vanilla
½ cup (1 stick) butter, melted
1 cup white flour
2 ripe pears, peeled and sliced or enough to cover the bottom of a 10-inch baking dish
Apple cider (about ¼ cup)
Ground cloves

Preheat oven to 400. In a large bowl, beat the eggs and gradually add the sugar. Add vanilla and butter and beat until well combined; slowly add flour. Arrange pear slices in the bottom of a greased 10-inch baking dish and cover with apple cider. Generously sprinkle with ground cloves. Spoon dollops of batter over the pears, baking will evenly distribute the batter. Bake for 20 minutes or until light brown and bubbly.

# AUTUMN APPLE CRISP

## Serves 6

A traditional favorite.

4    cups sliced tart apples, about 4 large
¼    cup orange juice
¾    cup sugar
¾    cup flour
½    teaspoon cinnamon
¼    teaspoon nutmeg
½    cup butter, (1 stick) semi-soft and cut into chunks

Preheat oven to 375. Oil a 9-inch pie plate and arrange apples evenly in the dish, pour orange juice over apples. In a medium bowl, combine sugar, flour, cinnamon and nutmeg; drop chunks of butter into flour mixture and with your fingers incorporate the butter with the flour until mixture is course. Sprinkle mixture over apples. Bake for 45 minutes.

# Dog Treats

Our Norwich terrier, Artichoke enjoys eating the dog biscuits in this chapter as much as I love making them for him. We always take them as a gift whenever we are invited to a dog/people outing. His friends love them too!

Artichoke's Favorite Dog Biscuits
Barley Flour Biscuits
Peanut Butter Dog Biscuits
Whole Wheat Dog Biscuits

# ARTICHOKE'S FAVORITE DOG BISCUITS

## Yields 4-5 dozen*

Our Norwich terrier, Artichoke loves these dog biscuits, as do his doggie friends. The dough is dense and compact. It is easier to roll at room temperature and also helpful if rolled between two sheets of wax paper. Feel free to use any size cutter or cut them into squares for a quick hassle free shape. Both the raw dough and the baked biscuits freeze well.

1    cup whole-wheat flour
1    cup white flour
½    cup soy flour (replace with rye flour if your dog is sensitive to digesting soy products)
¼    cup cornmeal
1    teaspoon salt
½    cup sunflower seeds, optional
2    tablespoons olive oil
¼    cup molasses
2    eggs, lightly beaten
¼    cup milk, any variety

Preheat oven to 325. In a large bowl, combine wheat flour, white flour, soy flour, cornmeal, salt and sunflower seeds. In a medium bowl, combine olive oil, molasses, eggs and milk; blend well. Add to dry ingredients. Knead for 2-3 minutes to fully incorporate the ingredients and let rest for 30 minutes. Roll dough out to *about* ¼ inch thickness and cut into desired shapes. Bake for 25-30 minutes. Turn off oven and allow biscuits to stay in oven for an additional 30 minutes.

\*    Yield based on a 1½ inch squares

# BARLEY FLOUR BISCUITS

# Yields about 4-5 dozen

This is an easy to prepare dog biscuit. Both the raw dough and the cooked biscuits freeze well.

| | |
|---|---|
| 1 | cup white flour |
| 1 | cup wheat flour |
| ½ | cup non-fat dry milk powder |
| ½ | cup raw wheat germ |
| ½ | cup barley flour |
| 1 | tablespoon brown sugar |
| 1 | egg, lightly beaten |
| 2 | tablespoons olive oil |
| ½-¾ | cup water |

Preheat oven to 325. In a large bowl, combine white flour, wheat flour, dry milk powder, wheat germ, barley flour and brown sugar. Stir in egg, olive oil and ½ cup water and combine to make a stiff dough, add the remaining ¼ cup water if dough is too dry. Knead for a few minutes and turn out to a floured board, roll to a ½ inch thickness and cut into desired shapes. Bake biscuits in a 325 oven for 30 minutes.

# PEANUT BUTTER DOG BISCUITS

## Yields about 6 dozen 1½ inch round biscuits

This biscuit is a favorite among dogs who love peanut butter. These biscuits freeze beautifully.

1½ cups whole-wheat flour
½ cup wheat germ
1 tablespoon brown sugar
¼ cup raisins, optional
1¼ cups smooth peanut butter
¾ cup milk, any variety

Preheat oven to 400. Line a cookie sheet with parchment paper. In a medium bowl combine wheat flour, wheat germ, brown sugar, and raisins. In a large mixing bowl with an electric beater, beat together peanut butter and milk on a low speed. Gradually add flour mixture, stirring with a spoon, mix until well combined. Dough will be *very* stiff, knead for about a minute. Roll out to a ¼ inch thickness and cut into desired shapes. Bake for 12-15 minutes. Cool on wire rack.

# WHOLE WHEAT DOG BISCUITS

## Sixty 2-inch biscuits

A stiff dough, but also an easy dough to work with.

2½  cups whole wheat flour
¼   cup raw wheat germ
½   cup non-fat dry milk powder
½   teaspoon salt
6    tablespoons canola oil
1    egg, lightly beaten
1    tablespoon molasses
½   cup cold water

Preheat oven to 375. In a large bowl, combine whole wheat flour, wheat germ, dry milk powder and salt. Add oil, egg, molasses and water; knead dough a few times or until ingredients are fully incorporated. Roll dough out to a ¼ inch thickness cut into desired shapes and bake for 20 minutes.

# Index

**Mozzarella**
Melted Cheese and
Artichokes, 21
Vegetarian Delight, 60
**Muenster Cheese Bread,
130**
**Parmesan**
Artichoke and Feta Melt,
10
Baked Spinach with
Cheese, 59
Melted Cheese and
Artichokes, 21
Polenta Lasagna, 114
Summertime Tomato Pie, 77
Vegetarian Delight, 60
**Ricotta**
Polenta Lasagna, 114
Smoked Salmon Pate, 8
Stuffed Chicken Breasts, 95
**Roquefort**
Marinated Roquefort, 5
Pesto Cheese Torte, 19
Red Cabbage Salad, 50
**Saga Cheese**
Pecan Blue Cheese Crack-
ers, 12
**Swiss**
Melted Swiss Dip, 3
Pistachio Gruyere Cheese
Spread, 15
Superb Zucchini Casse-
role, 112
Cheese Casserole, 76
Cheese Curry Pate with Plum
Sauce, 1
Cherries
Cherry Cobbler, 189
Cherry Cobbler, 189
**Chicken**
Chicken Soup with Corn-
meal Dumplings, 43

Creamy Chicken and Zuc-
chini Casserole, 80
Ginger Glazed Chicken, 106
Peanut Butter Soup with
Vegetables, 39
Stuffed Chicken Breasts, 95
Tofu, Leek and Prune Soup, 46
Wedding Soup, 34
Chicken Soup with Cornmeal
Dumplings, 43
Chili, 113
Chili Rellenos Casserole, 104
Chipped Beef and Cheese with
Walnuts, 7
Chocolate Beet Cake, 156
Chocolate Bread Pudding, 159
Chocolate Chip Peanut Butter
Bars, 161
**Chocolate Chips**
Chocolate Bread Pudding,
159
Chocolate Chip Peanut
Butter Bars, 161
Chocolate Covered Rice
Crispies, 166
Chocolate Meringue Pie, 167
Chocolate Oatmeal Crunch,
168
Creamy Chocolate Baby
Cakes, 163
Mysterious Butter Crunch,
165
Stay-Up-All-Night Cookies,
185
Yum Yum Dessert, 157
Chocolate Covered Rice
Crispies, 166
Chocolate Meringue Pie, 167
Chocolate Oatmeal Crunch, 168
Chocolate Truffles, 162
**Cocoa**
Buttermilk Cake, 160